MARY QUEEN OF SCOTS

Philip Ardagh writes both fiction and non-fiction, and is a familiar face at book festivals in England, Ireland, Scotland and Wales. His books have been translated into numerous languages, including Latin.

Alan Rowe lives in Surrey with his long-suffering partner and three noisy children where he draws silly pictures for a living. He also plays football, collects toys and refuses to grow up.

Mike Phillips is big, bald and blooming good fun. He lives in Essex with his wife and three children, illustrating books from his garden shed.

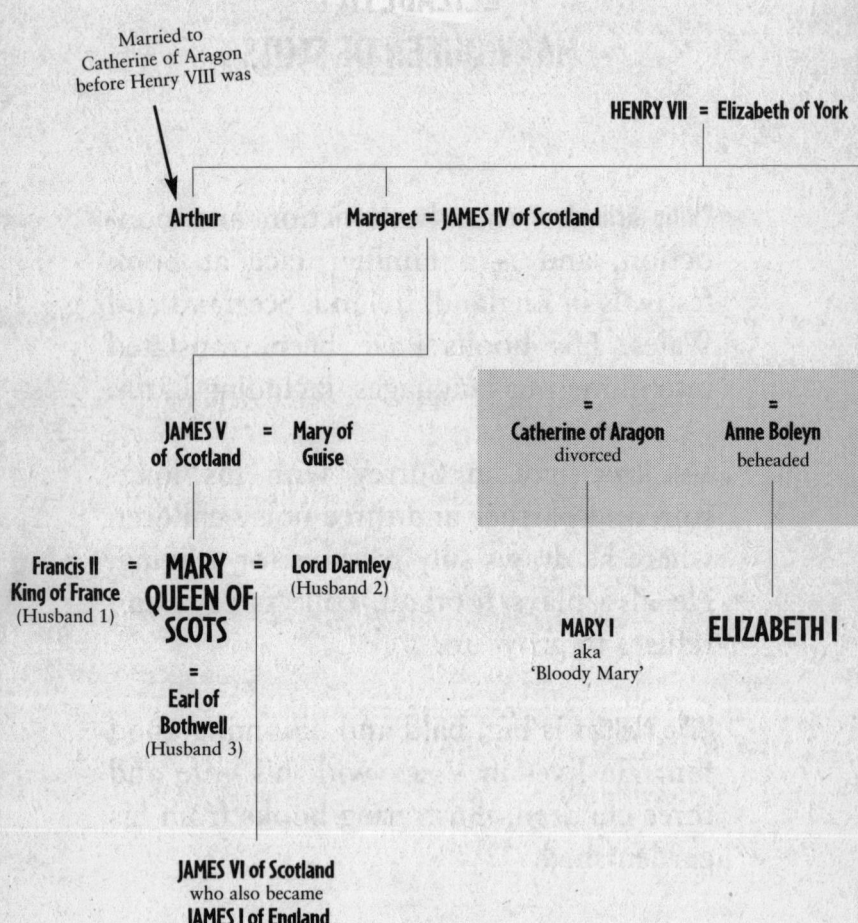

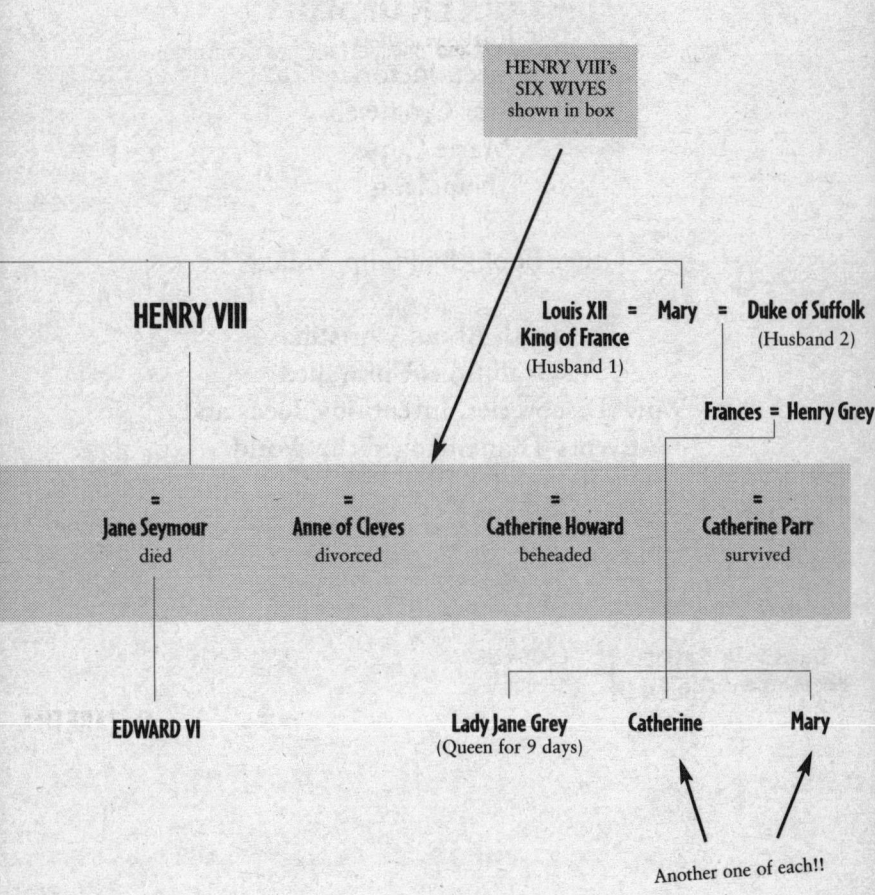

Books in the GET A LIFE! series

Julius Caesar
Queen Victoria
Oliver Cromwell
Marie Curie
Napoleon

Other Books by Philip Ardagh

The Truth About Christmas –
Its Traditions Unravelled
Wow! Discoveries, Inventions, Ideas and
Events That Changed the World

GET A LIFE!
HENRY VIII
ELIZABETH I
MARY QUEEN OF SCOTS

PHILIP ARDAGH

Illustrated by Alan Rowe and Mike Phillips

MACMILLAN CHILDREN'S BOOKS

For my editor, Gaby Morgan, for being nice to big men with beards; for Beany, the queen of our household; and for Francesca and Isabelle Laidlaw, with all that Scottish blood in their veins.

Henry VIII and Elizabeth I first published 1999 by Macmillan Children's Books
Mary Queen of Scots first published 2000 by Macmillan Children's Books

This edition published 2002 by Macmillan Children's Books
a division of Macmillan Publishers Limited
20 New Wharf Road, London N1 9RR
Basingstoke and Oxford
www.panmacmillan.com

Associated companies throughout the world

ISBN 0 330 39905 5

Copyright © Philip Ardagh 1999, 2000
Illustrations copyright © Mike Phillips 1999, 2000, Alan Rowe 1999

The right of Philip Ardagh to be identified as the
author of this book has been asserted by him in accordance
with the Copyright, Designs and Patents Act 1988.

All rights reserved. No part of this publication may be
reproduced, stored in or introduced into a retrieval system, or
transmitted, in any form, or by any means (electronic, mechanical,
photocopying, recording or otherwise) without the prior written
permission of the publisher. Any person who does any unauthorized
act in relation to this publication may be liable to criminal prosecution
and civil claims for damages.

1 3 5 7 9 8 6 4 2

A CIP catalogue record for this book is available from the British Library.

Typeset by Nigel Hazle
Printed and bound in great Britain by Mackays of Chatham plc, Kent.

CONTENTS

Henry VIII ix

Elizabeth I 57

Mary Queen of Scots 115

Timeline 175

GET A LIFE!
HENRY VIII

USEFUL WORDS
(and some rather silly ones too)

Here are some words you might come across when reading about Henry, and those silly ones I promised!

Annulled Cancelled out. Having a marriage annulled was officially saying that it was never really a marriage in the first place. Ooops!

Beheaded Having your head chopped off. Should really be *de*headed, if you think about it.

Cardinal A member of the Sacred College of the Roman Catholic Church, second only in importance to the Pope. So there!

Coffers Chests that money and valuables were kept in. 'England's coffers' is another name for England's Treasury ... often empty.

Cunning Man A bit like the local village witch doctor, who was supposed to solve petty crimes by using magic!

Excommunication Being cut off by the Church, so you're an outcast and not even allowed to pray.

Filchman A very large walking stick – more of a pole really – and ideal for hitting people with.

Heresy An opinion that's different from the view of the official Church.

Tudors Members of Elizabeth's family. Tudor was her family's last name, just like the Smith, Bloggs and Ardagh families' last names are Smith, Bloggs and Ardagh. (A Tudor house, for example, is a house built when one of the Tudor family was on the throne – from Henry VII in 1485 to Elizabeth's death in 1603.)

Tyburn A place in London where executions took place. Most victims were hanged – people are 'hanged', pictures are 'hung' – but some of the more important ones (people, not pictures) were beheaded instead.

BORN TO BE KING

Henry VIII's family name was Tudor. The 'VIII' bit is just Latin for 'eight' – a five (V) and three ones (III). The number eight simply tells us that there were seven other King Henrys on the English throne sometime before him. Henry's dad (Henry VII), for example, was King of England, but his grandfather wasn't. So how did the Tudor family end up with the English crown?

OWE IT TO OWEN

Back in 1415, the King of England was another man called Henry – Henry V this time, but certainly not a Tudor. Henry V is famous for leading the English army into battle that year, against the French at a place called Agincourt. Fighting for the English was a Welshman called Owen Tudor. (That last name sound familiar now, does it?) The English army of 5,700 defeated the French army of 25,000. Henry V then married a French princess called Catherine of Valois and they had a son. When the boy was just nine months old, Henry V died and the boy became king.

ANOTHER HENRY!

With her son Henry VI (the sixth) officially on the throne, Catherine heard rumours that a clerk of the wardrobe – that was a job title, not a piece of furniture – was secretly dating one of her ladies-in-waiting at the court. This was very naughty and certainly not allowed, so she went to confront him ... but ended up marrying him instead. The man's name? Why, Owen Tudor, of course! This caused BIG TROUBLE. Catherine should have got permission before doing something like that, so those ruling on behalf of the young king sent Catherine to a convent and threw Owen Tudor into Newgate Jail. He managed to escape twice and was recaptured twice.

BOUNCING BABIES

This didn't stop Catherine and Owen from having four children, though. And those children had 'royal blood' in them. After all, Catherine was the mother of King Henry VI, wasn't she, and had even been queen herself. Their dad, Owen Tudor, meanwhile, was pardoned, released from jail and became a royal park keeper back in Wales! Fifty years later – after winning the Wars of the Roses – Owen Tudor's grandson (our Henry VIII's dad) was able to claim the crown of England (as Henry VII) as his prize and Henry VIII followed him. All thanks to Owen Tudor, ex-soldier, ex-prisoner and park keeper.

THE WARS OF THE ROSES

This war was between two great 'houses' of England. Not the bricks-and-mortar kind of houses, but important families and their supporters. On one side were the Yorkists, with their emblem of the white rose, and on the other were the Lancastrians, with their red rose emblem. Henry VIII's father, Henry VII, was a Tudor from the House of Lancaster. When he became king, he married Elizabeth of York and created the emblem of the Tudor rose – both red and white. So, in a way, both the Lancastrians *and* the Yorkists won!

IT'S A BOY!

Henry VIII – who I'll call just plain 'Henry' from now on (but will give all the other Henrys their numbers or titles) – was born on 28 June 1491 at Greenwich Palace. He had a big brother called Arthur, who was Prince of Wales and the heir to the throne. Henry's title (apart from being a prince) was Duke of York. When, in 1502, Arthur died Henry was suddenly next in line to be king.

AN EDUCATION

Because Henry was a prince, it meant that he didn't have to go to school. (Hoorah!) But it didn't mean that he got out of having lessons. (Boo! Hiss!) He had his own private tutor called John Skelton. Skelton was a priest and a poet and always wore black robes. Unusually for teachers in those days, he didn't beat Henry much. Sometimes, a nobleman named Lord Mountjoy helped teach Henry too. Henry learnt everything from French and Latin to warfare, chess, dancing and card playing! There were very few books around, because printing had only just been invented.

SUPER DAD

Henry's dad, Henry VII, was a very good king. Uniting the houses of York and Lancaster had been a clever move when he'd married Elizabeth of York, and he did plenty of other smart things too. He made the powerful families of England less powerful, taking away their right to have huge private armies of their own. The only army in England should be the *king's* army, which made peace a much more likely prospect. Henry's dad also did a lot for law and order for ordinary people, creating justices of the peace and (less popular) official tax collectors.

THE YOUNG KING

Following his father's death on 21 April 1509, Henry became 'Henry VIII', aged just seventeen. Today most people think of Henry VIII as being fat and bearded, but it's important to remember that, when he first became king, he was slim, dashing and even thought to be good-looking. In fact, some people compared him to Alexander the Great!

HENRY'S FIRST QUEEN

Between becoming king and being crowned at his coronation, Henry married his long-time sweetheart and fiancée, Catherine of Aragon. This was just the sort of smart thing his father would have done. Catherine was the daughter of the King of Spain, and Spain was a very powerful country. This match would be good for England. Catherine of Aragon had been married to Henry's brother Arthur. When Arthur died, she'd become engaged to Henry . . . even though he was only twelve at the time! Now he was older, they got married less than two weeks before the coronation. This way Henry's bride could be crowned queen at the same time that he was crowned king.

CROWNING THE NEW KING

Henry was crowned on 23 June 1509. Rising at 6.00 a.m., he had a bath (which was extremely unusual), went to mass, then dressed in his finest clothes which included a crimson shirt and jacket of finest satin, covered with a fur-edged coat, also bright crimson. On his head was a little cap, later swapped for the crown. The coronation took place at Westminster Abbey and everyone wore fabulous robes and dresses. It was the brightest, best and richest-looking public spectacle the country had seen.

FUN, FUN, FUN

Now that Henry was king, he wanted life at the royal court to be fun, fun, fun. He loved his wife – kings often married for reasons other than love, remember – and he loved food, drink, hunting, gambling, singing and dancing and a whole host of other things. His father might have been a good king, but Henry thought him pretty B-O-R-I-N-G. Henry and Catherine moved from palace to palace (that's Greenwich, Richmond, Westminster and Windsor, not forgetting the Tower of London) having party after party!

BEHIND THE SCENES

Such serious partying needed a great deal of organization, and that was down to Henry's Lord Steward. Steward wasn't a name, but a title. A steward was in charge of all the eating arrangements and, for Henry's Lord Steward, that could mean banquets for 1,000 guests. Luckily for the Lord Steward, he had a staff of about five hundred men, women and children to help. (Queen Catherine, alone, had about 160 people looking after her!)

NOT SUCH FUN FOR SOME

Life wasn't one non-stop party for all Henry's officials and courtiers, though. Starting as he meant to go on, he had Edmund Dudley and Sir Richard Empson beheaded. (Yup, off with their heads!) They'd been his father's taxmen and no one liked paying tax much, so Henry knew that this would be a very popular move. Of course, he could simply have taken their jobs away from them, but this was much more fun!

HOW THE OTHER HALF LIVED

It was during Henry's reign that people began to build grand houses out of brick. Before that, the grandest houses had been built from stone, and before that, timber and wattle and daub (sticks, plaster and animal dung). If Henry visited a house and really liked it, he would persuade the owner to present it to him as a gift. It didn't take much persuasion because you couldn't really refuse a king . . . especially a king who'd already beheaded a few people. The most famous building he acquired that way was Hampton Court, from a man named Thomas Wolsey.

A MAN CALLED WOLSEY

Henry wasn't really interested in details. He wanted things done, but he happily left someone else to do the actual doing. At the start of his reign, that someone was a man named Cardinal Thomas Wolsey. As Lord Chancellor, Wolsey took care of the day-to-day details of government, which made him very powerful indeed. Wolsey's big failing was that he liked to show off as much as Henry himself, which was a very dangerous thing to do. Like the king, Wolsey loved money and possessions and dressing in fine clothes. He even wanted to be Pope – the head of the whole

Roman Catholic Church and one of the most important people in the western world!

THE MAN IN RED

Cardinals often wore red at official functions – it was a bit like a uniform – but Thomas Wolsey liked to wear red all the time, including a cap on his head. Of course, there were different shades of red to choose from, and he liked scarlet or crimson... made of the very finest of satin, which he could well afford. This probably clashed a bit with the orange pomander he often carried around with him. Yes, orange as in the *fruit*... though it wasn't always the same orange. It was stuck with cloves and God-knows-what, and was supposed to hide the nasty smells of everyday life in Henry's time. (Wolsey would give it a jolly good sniff when out and about amongst common people!)

SHOW OFF TO THE WORLD

Henry was eager to show the world that England was an important country and that he was an important king. He wanted to find an impressive way of showing off the country's wealth and importance to others. In 1520, a tournament was arranged on the continent, near Calais (which was English-owned). There were splendid tents and one was made of golden cloth, giving the event its name: *The Field of the Cloth of Gold*.

THE FIELD OF THE CLOTH OF GOLD

Over 5,000 people sailed over from England for the month-long tournament of free wine and entertainment. (There were fountains of wine. Literally.) The highlight of the tournament was supposed to be the meeting between Henry and Francis I, King of France, on 7 June 1520. They both pretended that the event was designed to create an important understanding between their two countries. It was really an excuse to see who could be the most extravagant and stylish – the show-offs!

NO FIGHTING PLEASE

Tournaments included jousts between knights and noblemen, but it was agreed that the two kings would not fight, just meet. And meet they did, both dressed in the latest stunning fashions. Henry wore gold and silver – and so did his horse, to match! Two weeks of English and French festivities followed, with plenty of singing and dancing. Despite the 'no fighting' agreement, Henry then went and spoilt everything by insisting on a quick wrestle . . . which he promptly lost! In next to no time, the loyal English were accusing Francis I of cheating (for how else could a Frenchman have won?) and things turned a little sour.

SECRET TALKS

The truth be told, Henry wasn't a great fan of the French king anyway. Part way through the month-long tournament, he'd snuck back over to England and met up with Emperor Charles V, Catherine of Aragon's nephew. Charles V was ruler of the Holy Roman Empire. I'm certainly not the first person to point this out – and I certainly won't be the last – but it's worth making it clear that the Holy Roman Empire wasn't holy, wasn't Roman and wasn't even really an empire. It was a group of small, squabbling German states, but 'Holy Roman Empire' sounded good. Talking of good, Charles V was also now King of Spain, for good measure, and *hated* Francis I of France. He and Henry signed a treaty 'of common cause' against the French. By 1522, England and France were at war once more.

A VICTORY . . . OF SORTS

Siding with Charles V seemed a smart move. In 1525, the forces of the Holy Roman Empire not only defeated the French at Pavia but also captured King Francis of France himself! Wolsey was quick to take advantage of the situation, and proposed that Henry march his army into Paris . . . an idea which Charles was less than thrilled by. It was mainly the Holy Roman Empire's money and soldiers that had been poured into the war, and Charles wasn't about to hand over French lands to Henry for his limited help!

FABULOUS FORCES

England then switched sides. It was Wolsey's idea, of course, because he was eager to be all-powerful in Europe. If Charles wasn't happy about Henry and England keeping Paris, he argued, then Henry should simply become his enemy! The head of the Roman Catholic Church was Pope Clement VII, and Wolsey was one of his cardinals. (Don't forget that England was a Roman Catholic country at the time.) Wolsey met with the Pope and others who

were fed up with Charles having so much power. They hatched a plot against the Holy Roman Empire. When Francis of France was released in 1526, he too joined the plot. For the first time in ages, England and France were on the *same* side. (GASP!)

A BAD MOVE

Charles V was no pushover, despite his powerful enemies. In May 1527, his troops ran amok in Rome, and even though no one would dare officially take Pope Clement VII prisoner, that's pretty much what he became. In 1529, the French hurriedly made peace with Charles, having suffered yet more defeats. Fortunately for them, Charles didn't occupy France, because he now had control over most of continental Europe. Much to Wolsey's embarrassment, England was ignored ... It obviously wasn't worth the effort to invade!

A RUDE AWAKENING

It must have been about then that Henry realized the terrible truth (shudder). His man Wolsey had led him to believe that England was a very important player on the European stage. (In other words, if events in Europe were in a play, England – and Henry – would get one of the biggest parts, with the best lines and some good action sequences.) It now turned out that Europe – and the likes of Charles V – could do what they liked without him ... (In this version of the play, Henry might be off-stage doing the catering.) And all Wolsey's time and effort (and England's coffers) being spent wheeling and dealing in European matters had another effect. Things had been left to go wrong at home.

GREAT HARRY

At the start of his reign, Henry had known that it wouldn't be long before England and France were at war again. It was traditional. They always seemed to be fighting each other. Perhaps it was because they were only separated by the Channel, so France was just a short cruise away ... Anyway, Henry wanted to strengthen the English army and be prepared. At the same time, he wanted to build a bigger, better navy. Not him personally, of course. Wolsey did a lot of the organizing. Henry's new navy had some super-sized ships in it. The biggest, called *Great Harry*, could carry 260 sailors and 400 soldiers, and weighed 1,000 tons. But this cost money ... Money which was not being spent on matters close to home.

THE MARY ROSE

Henry's most famous ship was the Mary Rose, but it's famous for the wrong reason. It sank! In 1545, the French were planning to invade England – surprise, surprise – and their ships appeared off the coast near Portsmouth. The massive Mary Rose sailed out to meet the enemy, which turned and ran (or whatever it is that ships do). Turning to sail triumphantly back to harbour, the Mary Rose capsized, drowning almost 500 men. Despite Henry's efforts, the ship lay at the bottom of the sea for over 430 years, until parts of it were salvaged in 1982.

A COSTLY BUSINESS

War was expensive, and not just in the loss of human lives (which wasn't Henry's main worry anyway). Records show that, between Henry coming to the throne in 1509 and the date of 12 June 1513, the Treasury had paid out over one million pounds ... and that didn't all go on partying. Far from it, in fact. Nearly 70 per cent of it was spent on war ... nearly half of which was spent *in one week,* in preparation to fight the French! More money was needed and, in 1523, Wolsey tried to raise this with his 'Amicable Grant'.

THE NOT-SO-AMICABLE GRANT

'Amicable' means friendly, but there was nothing friendly about the Amicable Grant – which wasn't really a grant either, it was a tax. All in all, it might have been a teeny-weeny bit more honest for Wolsey to have called it the Unpopular Tax, because that's what it was. If you owned property, you paid the tax to help pay for the war. There was uproar. People just didn't want to pay. Many people couldn't afford to anyway, and it looked like things were about to turn very nasty. With reports of possible armed rebellion in Kent and East Anglia, Henry cancelled the Amicable Grant saying that he'd never authorized it. Not only that, he automatically pardoned anyone who'd refused to pay Wolsey ... which was more than a public humiliation for the cardinal. It was also a reminder to Wolsey of who was really boss.

GONE TO HIS HEAD?

Wolsey certainly liked power. He's famous for starting out by issuing orders which began with 'the King says', later changing that to 'we say' and, finally, 'I say'. The power had gone to his head. He'd done rather well for himself from being a butcher's (and a Mrs Butcher's) son to a cardinal to Lord Chancellor, too. He was also very rich. Rumours spread that he'd used the king's money to build up his own personal fortune. In fact, he'd used money from the Church... and matters of the Church were to be his downfall.

A MARRIAGE ON THE ROCKS

Sad to say, but Henry didn't love his wife any more. Catherine of Aragon was five years older than him, approaching forty (which seemed a lot older in those days than it does now, because people died much younger then), and getting a bit dumpy and wrinkled. Now, there's nothing wrong with being dumpy or wrinkled, or both for that matter, except that Henry didn't like it. To make matters worse, Catherine had 'failed' to give him a healthy son.

THE TRAGEDY OF CATHERINE'S CHILDREN

Henry and Catherine of Aragon's first child, a daughter, was stillborn. Their next three children were either sickly and died, or were stillborn. Finally, poor Catherine gave birth to a healthy child on 18 February 1516. Henry had her

christened Mary after his favourite sister. (She later earned the name 'Bloody Mary', but I'll save the reason why for another time.)

GOOD GOD!

Despite all the fun partying, Henry and Catherine were enthusiastic Catholics. But, after ten years on the throne of England and much praying and promises to God, there was no male heir – no prince to become king should Henry die. Then Henry had been naughty-naughty and had an affair with one of Catherine's ladies-in-waiting, by the name of Elizabeth Blount. They saw a lot of each other and, in 1519, had a healthy bouncing baby boy. In Henry's mind, that proved that the lack of sons in his marriage to Catherine was his *wife's* 'fault', not his!

A GOOD CATHOLIC . . . SOMETIMES

In Germany, a man named Martin Luther had broken away from the Catholic faith and was preaching what was seen as heresy – against the teachings of the Church. He published a book full of his ideas in 1520. In 1521, a book appeared in London called 'The Defence of the Seven Sacraments' which argued for the Church and against Luther. It was a best-seller all over Europe . . . and Henry had written it! He even dedicated it to the Pope. In recognition of this, on 11 October 1521, the Pope gave Henry the title 'Defender of the Faith'. Despite everything that was to follow (and, boy, was there lots to follow), Henry was proud of the title until the day he died.

ANNE BOLEYN

Elizabeth Blount was no longer at the royal court and Henry had a new mistress called Mary Boleyn. Mary had a great deal of influence over the king and persuaded him to make her sister, Anne, one of the queen's ladies-in-waiting. Anne Boleyn's eyes are said to have been 'black and beautiful', and she had *six* fingers on one hand. She also had a number of admirers, including the poet Sir Thomas Wyatt and Henry Percy, son of the Earl of Northumberland. Anne obviously liked Percy and might have married him . . . except for Cardinal Wolsey sticking his nose in and putting an end to it. This was probably on Henry's instructions.

DO THE RIGHT THING!

It soon became clear that Henry was more interested in Anne than Mary Boleyn, but the king was in for a shock. When he made his royal advances towards her, she made it clear that she had no wish to be a royal mistress, but would happily be his wife! She then left the royal court and went back to her family home at Hever Castle in Kent . . . This was a smart move because a great way of making Henry want something even more was to say that he couldn't have it. He was KING, wasn't he? He bombarded her with love letters.

THE ILLEGITIMATE HEIR

Henry loved the son he'd had by Elizabeth Blount. He had christened him Henry Fitzroy after himself and, when the boy was six, made him Duke of Richmond. There was even talk of finding him a foreign princess to marry and it was

made clear that, if Henry had no legitimate son, this boy would become king after him. Even Catherine agreed to this in public. Amazingly, Pope Clement VII was even prepared to let Henry Fitzroy marry Henry and Catherine's daughter – his own half-sister – to cement his right to England's crown!!! But Henry still wanted a legitimate heir, to be sure that no one could dispute the Tudors' right to sit on the throne of England for many generations ... and Anne Boleyn wanted to marry Henry, so the choice seemed simple. Henry must divorce Catherine, marry Anne, and he and his new wife would have a son.

THE KING'S GREAT MATTER

Henry gave Cardinal Wolsey the job of getting an official annulment of the marriage between him and Catherine of Aragon. The Roman Catholic Church doesn't allow divorce, but does allow annulments under very special circumstances. As a cardinal of Rome, Wolsey set up a secret tribunal to 'charge' Henry with being unlawfully married to Catherine. The excuse they dreamt up for the marriage being 'unlawful' was that Henry had married his brother's wife ... the fact that his brother was *dead* didn't come into it. Catherine wasn't aware of the tribunal and neither was the Pope, but Wolsey intended to annul the marriage then convince him to agree to it. The whole thing was a fudge! Then the Pope was more or less kidnapped by Catherine's nephew Charles V, whom I mentioned back on page 15, and the whole thing had to be dropped.

THE CRAFTY CARDINAL

Now Thomas Wolsey switched to Plan B. He would try to convince the Pope that, as long as he was being held by Charles V, he should pass his authority on to someone else ... and that this 'acting pope' should be none other than himself: Cardinal Wolsey! Unfortunately for the cardinal, on 22 June 1527, Henry made the mistake of telling Catherine of Aragon that he thought that they hadn't been properly married for the past eighteen years! Wolsey had expected the king not to say anything until the marriage had been successfully annulled. Now the secret was out, and Catherine sent a message to her nephew Charles V.

A VERY PUBLIC PROBLEM

Suddenly, Henry's private wedding difficulties were the talk of Europe. Not only that, Charles V wrote to Aunt Catherine offering her his full support as well as informing Clement VII (his prisoner, the Pope) that he should consider removing Wolsey's powers. Henry himself was getting fed up with Wolsey, particularly because the cardinal seemed to think that Henry's next wife should be a French noblewoman called Renée ... He didn't think Anne Boleyn was suitable!

THE CARDINAL COCKS UP

While Cardinal Wolsey was in Europe in 1527, trying to whip up support for him to be made 'acting pope', Henry asked the Pope directly if he would not only annul his marriage to poor old Catherine, but also give the thumbs-up to him marrying Anne Boleyn. When Wolsey returned to England, he found the king a changed man. Suddenly, Henry *liked* doing things for himself. In the past, he'd signed any letter Wolsey put in front of him without even bothering to read it. Not any more. Not only that, Wolsey was only allowed to see Henry when Anne Boleyn agreed to it!

BACK IN FAVOUR

Henry's approaches to Pope Clement VII were a complete flop. Wolsey, however, had an unexpected success. The Pope suddenly agreed to let the whole affair be sorted out in England by another cardinal called Lorenzo Campeggio. Once a friend of Henry's, as well as being a cardinal Campeggio was also Bishop of Salisbury. Matters should soon be sorted out, so long as everyone survived the plague . . .

THE PLAGUE

In 1528, the 'sweating sickness' was particularly bad in England, and London was one of the easiest places to catch it. Henry was convinced that he'd get it so fled London and kept on the move. He attended at least three masses a day, wrote several wills and kept trying all the quack medicines that were supposed to protect one. He'd left Anne Boleyn at court . . . and she hadn't been looking too well when he'd fled. What a caring guy!

ILLNESS AND ACCIDENTS

Henry had many illnesses and accidents in his life. In 1514 he'd had smallpox (which was often a killer). In 1521, he caught malaria from a mosquito bite. In 1524 he forgot to put his visor down in a friendly joust and got bits of shattered lance in his face. In 1525, when out hawking, he tried to polevault across a ditch . . . but he was too heavy for the pole which snapped. He landed head first in the mud with such force that his head got stuck and he couldn't breath. He had to be rescued by a footman. Then, in 1528, an ulcer appeared on one of his legs, soon to be followed by many more on both of them. In the end, Henry was unable to walk at all. To top it all, he used to get horrible headaches!

TROUBLEMAKER

What our Henry had no way of knowing was that Cardinal Campeggio was on a mission of time-wasting! It usually took about six weeks to travel from Rome to England. This may sound a long time, but Campeggio took *four months*. Once he'd arrived, things got even worse. Instead of looking into the annulment, he announced that it was his duty to try to repair Henry and Catherine's broken marriage! Campeggio's special tribunal didn't open until 18 June 1529. That was eight months after he'd first arrived in London.

FROM BAD TO WORSE

If Henry had thought that, now the tribunal had opened, things might begin to go in his favour, he was sadly (and badly) mistaken! Catherine appeared in person and, kneeling at the king's feet, sobbed, 'For the love of God, let me have justice and right.' She then confronted Henry, saying that if he could prove she'd done anything unlawful, she was 'content to depart to my great shame and dishonour'. She then left the Blackfriars court. Henry was gobsmacked. Just over a month later, Campeggio adjourned the court until October!

WOLSEY LOSES OUT

Now everything was a complete and utter public mess and Henry blamed Cardinal Wolsey. Hadn't he been supposed to sort the matter out swiftly and secretly ages ago? Now Wolsey found that his usual rooms at court were occupied by someone else. He found that the king would rather go riding with Anne Boleyn than discuss important matters with him. On 22 September 1529, he was ordered to surrender the Lord Chancellor's great seal. (He was Lord Chancellor, so this was a bit like a cop being asked to hand in his badge.) Wolsey refused until he saw the king's handwriting on the order. He is said to have broken down and cried.

ESCAPING THE BLOCK

Henry wanted more than Wolsey's job off him, he wanted his life. The king was angry and, if he wasn't going to get his own way, at least Wolsey would pay for it. Wolsey would be tried, though everyone knew how that trial would end: at the executioner's block with Wolsey's severed head in a basket. But Henry was denied that. On 29 November 1530, Wolsey died in Leicester on the way to the trial. He was pompous to the end, saying that if he'd served God as well as he'd served Henry, God wouldn't have given him grey hairs!

LIFE AFTER WOLSEY

With Thomas Wolsey out of the way, Henry needed another Lord Chancellor and he wasn't about to choose another churchman. Instead, he chose another Thomas – Thomas More, this time. More was a lawyer, not a cardinal, and Henry had known him for years. Thomas More is famous for being called 'a man for all seasons'. In other words, he could be happy and funny, or serious and sad ... whatever was required of him. Unfortunately, he didn't always see eye to eye with his king.

JUST SAY 'NO'? NO

When Henry first offered Thomas More the job of Lord Chancellor, he said 'no'. He was a devout Roman Catholic and believed that Henry and Catherine of Aragon should stay married. But Henry wouldn't take 'no' for an answer. He said that More *must* take the job, but that he'd never be forced to do anything against his religious beliefs. The plans for divorce or annulment would be dealt with by other people. Thomas accepted the job.

ANY MORE, SIR THOMAS?

Historians with time on their hands before lunch sometimes divide Henry VIII's advisers into 'doers' and 'thinkers'. Wolsey was certainly a 'doer' and Sir Thomas More a 'thinker' ... but More did some 'doing' too. In fact, he took part in drawing up forty-four articles listing all the terrible things Cardinal Wolsey was supposed to have done. He also found time to write books, including a couple on heresy, which is any opinion which differs from the view of the official Church. Of course, the official Church in England was still the Catholic Church. When that changed, More's views on heresy proved far less popular, even dangerous ... for him.

YET ANOTHER THOMAS

When it came to sorting out the mess with Catherine of Aragon, Henry called in yet *another* Thomas – and, yes, that does make things confusing. This Thomas was one Thomas Cromwell. His father was a blacksmith, but making horseshoes didn't interest Thomas. He left his father to it and went to Italy as a 'soldier of fortune' – pay him enough and he'd fight on your side. Later, he became a merchant and a lawyer. In 1520 he'd joined Wolsey's household, when Wolsey was possibly the most powerful man in England. He became a member of parliament in 1529, was a member of the Privy Council in 1531 and was a well-respected royal adviser. If this speedy rise in importance made him happy, it didn't show. He always looks gloomy in his portraits!

THE OTHER OTHER THOMAS

Another important Thomas in Henry's life was the churchman Thomas Cranmer. You'll find his name cropping up right to the very end. He was ordained a Roman Catholic priest in 1523, and in 1529 suggested that the question of Henry's marriage (or divorce) be looked at by the universities of Europe. Because this was a neat way of stopping the matter being left solely to the all-powerful Pope, Henry liked it. He liked Cranmer too.

CHANGING TACTICS

When Cardinal Campeggio announced that the whole marriage problem would have to be dealt with back in Rome, Henry decided that enough was enough. He was too proud a man to go and beg his cause to the Pope in person ... that would be on foreign soil. Here, in England, he was in charge. With Thomas Wolsey gone and Thomas More not involved, Henry took matters into his own hands. He would turn his subjects – the people of England – against the Church.

A STATE WITHIN A STATE

Like most Roman Catholic countries in Europe, much of England's land actually belonged to the Roman Catholic Church and so to Rome. A third of it did ... which was more than Henry himself owned! Many churchmen abused their power and wealth (as did many non-churchmen, of course), and some bishops earned more than England's top noblemen. (Noble*women* didn't earn anything. That was the way of the world back then.) As a result, many people – rich and poor – hated the Church, and Henry was about to use that hate to *his* advantage.

ABOVE THE LAW

What made the Church really unpopular were the tithes. These were taxes ordinary people had to pay to the Church for a whole variety of things. Tithes were based on a proportion of a person's income so even the very, very poor had to pay something. There were special Church courts that made sure you paid, or suffered if you didn't. They had nothing to do with the ordinary law of the land, and you couldn't appeal against a sentence. If that wasn't bad enough, if a clergyman (churchman) was accused of breaking the law, he could demand the right to be tried in a Church court instead of an ordinary one. Because he was tried by his friends and colleagues, more often than not he'd be found innocent!

ACTION AT LAST

Henry let it be known that he'd sort out the Church in England, getting rid of all the corruption and greed. This wasn't really his job – it was the Pope's – but he had parliament on his side. In 1529, pleased with their king's new approach, they sent him a petition. In it, they asked Henry to explain what 'laws of God' allowed churchmen to be greedy, have many jobs, buy and sell goods and live miles

> And there is absolutely NO evidence to suggest this poor hardworking priest stole your sheep...

away from the parishes of the people they were supposed to be caring for. A number of bishops had seats in the House of Lords. When they heard about the petition, it's said that they 'frowned and grunted'!

LAYING DOWN THE LAW

The king put forward three main demands. Firstly, that all future Church laws would have to receive the king's consent (in other words, be approved by him first). Secondly, a special royal commission would go through all the existing Church laws and decide which could or couldn't stay. Thirdly – and, boy, was this most importantly – that the Church in England got its power not from the Pope (or anyone else for that matter) but from the king. English bishops swore loyalty to the Pope in Rome. But shouldn't they be swearing loyalty to *him*? Henry reasoned.

A NEW WIFE

Although matters with the Church were still not sorted, Henry 'divorced' Catherine of Aragon and married the Marchioness of Pembroke on 25 January 1533, in secret. The Marchioness of *Who*? Oh sorry, didn't I tell you? Anne Boleyn had been getting so fed up waiting around to see whether she and Henry would ever get married, that Henry decided he'd better give her £1,000 a year and an important title. So in 1532, she became Marchioness of Pembroke. The reason why they got married the following January was that Anne was pregnant ... and, if the baby turned out to be a boy, Henry didn't want to run the risk of him being illegitimate.

This isn't how I imagined my wedding day would be!

Shhh! Keep your voice down! This is a secret ceremony.

AN AMAZING RESULT!

With a new (not-so-secret) secret wife and a baby on the way, Henry had to sort out 'the King's Great Matter' – as the business with the Church had become known – before the baby was born. Luck was on his side. The Archbishop of Canterbury died and the Pope's choice of new archbishop was none other than Henry's friend and adviser Thomas

Cranmer. On 23 May 1533, he agreed with Henry that his marriage to Catherine had been 'unlawful' because she'd been married to Henry's (now dead) brother first. In fact, in the eyes of the Church, they had never been married at all. This was the selfsame argument Wolsey had first put forward way, way back on page 23! Archbishop Cranmer then declared that the marriage between Henry and Anne Boleyn was legal and good.

CROWNING THE NEW QUEEN

Soon after, on a glorious summer's day, Anne Boleyn was crowned Queen of England. The streets were filled with people – of course they were; it was a public holiday with free drink – but very few of them threw their hats in the air or cheered. The truth be told, some even 'boo'-ed and shouted, 'Long live Queen Catherine!' Thomas More actually stayed at home.

A BASE FOR ROYAL POWER

Now that Cranmer had made it possible for Henry to remarry, it was down to Cromwell to give Henry absolute power over the Church and other matters. There followed a whole batch of parliamentary acts with such weird and wonderful names as *The Act of First Fruits and Tenths* and *The Act in Absolute Restraint of Annates,* but two of the most important ones were *The Treason Act* and *The Act of Succession*. The Act of Treason made it treason – punishable by death – to say that the king was a heretic. In other words, whatever Henry said about the Church was OK. In effect, he was now head of the Church in England.

THE ACT OF SUCCESSION

This dealt with the rather tricky subject of Henry's children. Now that his marriage to Catherine of Aragon had been declared not-a-marriage-after-all, their daughter Mary was officially declared illegitimate, as was Henry's son, Henry Fitzroy. Mary had no claim to the throne of England. Any children Henry and Anne Boleyn had would be heirs to the English crown.

BOUNCING BABY BESS

Much to Henry's disappointment, Anne Boleyn's baby turned out to be a girl. Born on 7 September 1533, they christened her 'Elizabeth', but little did anyone realize that she'd one day grow up to become queen. All Henry could think about back then was a legitimate son and heir.

ANOTHER TROUBLESOME LIZ

Another Elizabeth, this time Elizabeth Barton, was playing a very dangerous game. Known as the Holy Maid of Kent, she'd spoken out against Henry's plans to divorce Catherine in the past. Now she was saying that, having married Anne Boleyn, Henry would die a 'villain's death' in less than a month. A number of people believed Elizabeth Barton for two reasons: firstly, she had been miraculously cured of an incurable disease years before. Secondly, because she carried a golden letter sent down from heaven supporting her claims... at least her followers thought that was the case. (It does seem a little unlikely to me, though!) Henry wanted her executed but, for fear of upsetting her ever-growing following, he simply had her put in prison... and then hanged on 12 April 1534 when most people had forgotten about her.

THOMAS LOSES FAVOUR

Although he was for Catherine and against Henry's marriage to Anne Boleyn, Thomas More was careful not to side with the Holy Maid of Kent. He described her as a 'wicked woman'... but he too would soon end up dead. Henry's policy was along the lines of 'if you aren't with me you're against me' and More was being too wishy-washy. He just couldn't bring himself to swear to Henry's authority over the Church in England, so he ended up a prisoner in the Tower of London.

UNDER SENTENCE OF DEATH

When, in 1535, the Constable of the Tower, Sir William Kingston, heard that Thomas More was to be executed, he burst into tears. More told him to 'be of good cheer' and assured him that they'd all meet up again in heaven one day and 'be merry for ever and ever'. Henry had originally planned to have him horribly tortured before being executed, but he changed his mind. When Thomas More learnt of this, he made some joke about Henry being *so* merciful! He was then taken to the scaffold at Tyburn.

THE BEARD IS INNOCENT!

Thomas More had grown a long white beard whilst he was a prisoner in the Tower. Now he was resting his head on the executioner's block at Tyburn, he was careful to lift it free from his neck so that it trailed down the front of the block. Why? Because, as Thomas More himself declared, his beard 'had never committed treason'. Now it wouldn't get the chop when his neck did. He'd saved his beard's life!

WIFE NUMBER THREE PLEASE

Less than a year after Thomas More's bearded head was separated from his body, so was Anne Boleyn's beard-free head from hers. Not only had she 'failed' to give Henry the son he so badly wanted, but he'd also set his heart on a lady-in-waiting called Jane Seymour, and he didn't have to worry or give two figs about what the Church thought any more! After Anne was found guilty of seeing other men behind the king's back (which were probably completely made-up charges), she was executed on 19 May 1536. A razor-sharp sword wielded by a French executioner was used instead of the more usual axe. How considerate. She was the second of Henry's wives to die that year. His first, Catherine of Aragon, had died on 8 January, of natural causes.

'NO GREAT BEAUTY'

Unlike Anne, who'd encouraged the king's advances, Jane Seymour was described as being 'full of goodness' and an honest, straightforward lady. In fact, she even returned his letters unopened, refused gifts and wouldn't see him in private – all things which ended up making Henry chase after her even harder. The moment Henry heard that Anne had been executed, he visited Jane Seymour and they became engaged. By the end of the month (May 1536) they were married. Now Anne's daughter, Elizabeth, was officially illegitimate along with his first wife's daughter, Mary!

NAMING HIS HEIR

Henry wasn't getting any younger and, with all his accidents and ill health (see page 26), he was probably beginning to suspect that he might die before he had a son and heir. There was a clause in the Act of Succession which said that he could name his own heir to the throne if he didn't have a son by his latest wife (in this case Jane). He probably planned to appoint his illegitimate son Henry Fitzroy, Duke of Richmond, but, sadly for the king, the duke died. Henry had him buried in secret. Now Henry began to think the unthinkable . . . what if he made one of his daughters – a WOMAN – his heir?

BACK IN COURT

After being shunned, Henry's elder daughter Mary suddenly found herself back in favour. She was allowed back in court and, along with her half-sister, Elizabeth, was made welcome by Jane Seymour who became a kind stepmother to them both. Mary, however, remained a Roman Catholic like her mother Catherine before her.

DISSOLUTION OF THE MONASTERIES

Apart from being big and bearded, having six wives and having people's heads chopped off, Henry VIII is probably best known for the dissolution of the monasteries. This may sound more dull than the other things that I've just mentioned, but it had an enormous effect on England and helped raise HUGE AMOUNTS OF CASH for the king.

THE *VALOR ECCLESIASTICUS*

Way, way, way back in 1086 – which was still way (singular) back in Henry's time – the then King of England, William the Conqueror, ordered the compiling of the Domesday Book. This listed the property and land ownership of England. Now that Henry was the head of the Church in England, he wanted a similar kind of document listing all the *Church's* property and lands. It was drawn up by Thomas Cromwell in 1535 and was called *Valor Ecclesiasticus*.

A TREASURE TROVE

Jam-packed with detail, the report must have made mouth-watering reading for the cash-strapped king. All that land, those buildings and the treasures within those buildings now belonged to him . . . and what Henry needed most was M-O-N-E-Y. After all those parties when he'd first come to the throne and all the money spent on the army and navy and wars since then, here was a new, rich source of income. But what to do?

THE DISSOLUTION SOLUTION

I'll tell you what he did. He dissolved the monasteries – not in a giant vat of acid, but the result was pretty much the same. He threw out the monks, seized anything of value and let the buildings fall into disrepair. (They became a very useful source of building materials for new buildings and even farm walls. Why pay for stones when you could nip down the road and pinch them from an abandoned abbey or monastery?) Henry had done a great job in making the Church out to be the 'bad guy' so there wasn't much opposition. He'd start with the smaller monasteries and work up!

Very impressive, Your Majesty... but how will you dissolve the-er-BIGGER monasteries?

THE NAME'S BOND, VAGABOND

The countryside in Henry's day (and night) was pretty nasty. It wasn't all blue skies and pretty trees rustling in the gentle breeze. Most people were farmers or farmhands because you needed to grow food in order to have something to eat. The rich had huge farms. The poor farmed the common land that was for everyone ... The trouble was, the greedier the rich became, the more common land they fenced off for themselves, until there wasn't enough to go around. This left landless men roaming the countryside trying to find work, often stealing to stay alive. The rich saw them as landless louts and called them 'vagabonds'. To add to their number, there were now the hundreds of homeless monks left wandering about with nothing to do. So if you didn't run into a vagabond, you might well have met a monk.

TROUBLE UP NORTH

Trouble was brewing up in the north of England. There, people showed more loyalty to their lords and masters than to their king. Although the north was important because it was on the border with those wild and woolly Scots, Henry had never even been there. It was wild countryside and he'd heard that northerners were pretty wild too! Then, when Henry was enjoying rich festivities with Jane Seymour (Wife Number Three), at least partly paid for by those dissolved monasteries, there was a rebellion.

THE PILGRIMAGE OF GRACE

When Catherine of Aragon had still been queen, three powerful lords from the north – Thomas Dacre, Thomas Darcy and John Hussey – had plotted on her side and against the king. Now Catherine was out of the picture, they just plotted against the king in general! The closing of the monasteries was the last straw. A riot broke out in Lincolnshire on 1 October 1536 and spread, in pockets, across the country, but a much more serious uprising took place in York on 8 October. It was led by a one-eyed lawyer named Robert Aske, who claimed that his group of followers were on a pilgrimage.

MAKING DEMANDS!

Aske and his 'Pilgrims' were a 40,000-strong army with four main aims: Henry and Catherine of Aragon's daughter, Mary, should no longer be seen as illegitimate, the Pope should be accepted as the head of the Church in England and, thirdly, the Church should be given all its powers and property back. They even took it on themselves to reopen some of the local monasteries! The fourth aim was not a religious one. The Pilgrims wanted a proper parliament, one which represented the people and didn't simply agree to whatever the king wanted.

A MAN OF HONOUR

Henry's army was in such a pathetic state after years of fighting, that Aske's Pilgrim army could probably have marched into London and seized control. But Aske was an honourable man and he accepted Henry as his king (and a nice satin jacket as a present). When brought a promise of a parliament, and that none of his Pilgrims would be punished if they went to their homes, Aske agreed.

It's not a bribe, honestly... and you don't need to dry-clean it, whatever it says on the label.

A TURN FOR THE WORSE

Another rebel, this time a man called Bigod, whipped up support and, in February 1537, tried to take control of Hull and Scarborough. Unlike Aske and his Pilgrims of

Grace, he had always been *against* the Pope ... but after he was defeated and his supporters hanged on the king's orders (including the monks who had reoccupied their monastery in Sawley), Henry used it as an excuse to go back on his word and have Aske hanged too.

DAZZLING PALACES

To go with Hampton Court palace (formerly Cardinal Wolsey's home), Whitehall (once the palace of the Archbishop of York), Greenwich (where he was born), Bridewell, St James's, Eltham and Windsor – this is getting to be a long list, huh? – Henry used some of his new-found wealth to build Nonsuch. It was so big and so grand that he had a village – including its church – knocked down to make way for it! And where is it now? Nonsuch? No such place, I'm afraid. It's all gone.

A ROYAL PRINCE

Riches or no riches, what Henry wanted most was a baby boy – a son and heir who would become king after him and carry on the Tudor name – and, on 12 October 1537, that's what he got. Jane Seymour gave birth to little Edward at Hampton Court, but it was to kill her. Twelve feverish days after the joyous event, she died. Thrilled to have a prince at last, Henry was equally horrified by his queen's death. She lay in state for three weeks before being buried in St George's Chapel, Windsor, in great pomp and ceremony.

She was the only of Henry's six wives ever to receive such an honour.

NEW TROUBLE

Pope Clement VII had died in 1535. His successor, Paul III, had been pushed too far. On 17 December 1538, he issued a bull (an official declaration) stating that, although he'd excommunicated Henry from the Roman Catholic Church in an earlier bull (back in '35), he hadn't made it Church law, in the hope that Henry might see the error of his ways, repent and come back to the Church . . . Instead, Henry had done things such as digging up the bones of Saint Thomas à Becket, trying them for treason, then burning them and scattering the ashes! (He also used the 'dissolved' St Augustine's Abbey to keep deer in.) This meant WAR!

THE KINGS OF CHRISTENDOM!

Pope Paul now called upon all loyal Roman Catholics to rise up against Henry. He couldn't have the bull actually published in England itself, but he made sure that there were copies floating around in France, Scotland and Ireland so that some would filter through into Henry's kingdom soon enough. Now it was a matter of taking sides. The Pope wanted Emperor Charles (he of Holy Roman Empire and King of Spain fame) to end the war he was having with the Turks at the time, and to attack Henry instead. Charles suggested that the Pope try to get France to take action against Henry, since he was too busy. But he would try to suppress the Protestants in Germany who might otherwise fight on Henry's side. It was all getting jolly complicated!

CRAFTY CROMWELL

With Jane Seymour dead, Henry was single again. Cromwell reasoned, what better way to get a foreign power on England's side than to make one of their princesses Queen of England? Henry should have a foreign bride! Henry rather liked the idea because he thought there were plenty of pretty princesses to choose from. Having divorced his first wife and beheaded his second, the possible brides-to-be were probably less thrilled at the thought of it!

IN THE FRAME

In France, there wasn't only the king's daughter, Margaret, but also the Duke of Guise's daughter, Marie, to choose from. But King James V of Scotland had his eye on Marie and he married her instead. Meanwhile, our Henry turned his attention to Christina, Duchess of Milan. Milan was an important piece of territory wanted by both Emperor Charles and King Francis. If he married the duchess, he'd be in a powerful position. He had the famous painter Hans Holbein paint a portrait of Christina to bring back and show him, and he liked what he saw. But the marriage was not to be. Next, Holbein painted Marie (now Queen of Scotland)'s two sisters, Louise and Renée . . . but there were others to consider too.

While you're at it, could you paint a small version for my passport picture?

BEAUTY PARADE!

With so many possible brides out there in Europe, Henry decided to hold a kind of beauty parade for the 'hopefuls' in English-owned Calais. He suggested that the Queen of France could be there too, to make sure everything was conducted properly. King Francis didn't like the idea for a variety of obvious reasons. Not only was it *not* the done thing to parade women like horses in a show ring, but Francis was in secret meetings with his old enemy Charles and didn't want (anti-Charles) Henry to ruin everything.

WIFE NUMBER FOUR

By now, Cromwell was getting desperate to find Henry a foreign bride before the king got fed up with the idea not working as planned ... and he, Cromwell, got the blame! He told Henry of the 'beautiful' Anne of Cleves. Another Holbein portrait was painted and brought over to Henry, and he agreed to marry her. When she came to England, Henry was horrified. In his opinion, Anne was nothing like her portrait. He called her the Flanders mare – 'Flanders' being where she came from, and a 'mare' being a horse! Very reluctantly indeed (because he couldn't afford to offend the powerful families involved) he married poor Anne.

See if she'll settle for a stable far away from here and as much hay as she can eat.

AN AMICABLE ARRANGEMENT

Henry and Anne of Cleves just didn't really get along from the word go. So, by the following year, he'd managed to divorce her, throwing in a castle, a palace and a manor house, their flashy contents, an annual allowance and the rather odd title of 'the king's beloved sister'. Anne's (genuine) brother had wanted her to go back home, but Anne had grown to like England. She stayed on good terms with Henry and those who ruled after him. Dying in 1557, she was buried in Westminster Abbey.

CROMWELL GETS THE CHOP

Things might have stayed smiles between Anne and the king (relieved to get her off his hands) but they didn't stay so fine-and-dandy for Cromwell. Life seemed sweet for him. Henry made Cromwell the Lord Chamberlain of the Household in April 1540 but less than two months later he was arrested in the middle of a meeting around the Council table and stripped of his honours. Why? He was not only blamed for 'tricking' Henry into a loveless marriage to the 'Flanders mare' but – in a royal court where everyone was out to get everyone else – also accused of treason. If you think none of this makes any sense, think how poor old Thomas Cromwell must have felt! He wrote a letter to his king ending 'mercy, mercy, mercy', but mercy he did not get. What he *did* get was his head chopped off.

HOWDY HOWARD!

On the day Cromwell died, Henry married the beautiful Catherine Howard. Catherine was Anne Boleyn's cousin. Because of this, she showed an interest in Anne and Henry's daughter, Elizabeth. She even sat the princess at an important place during a feast to celebrate her marriage. To begin with, Henry thought his new – and very young – bride to be his 'blushing rose without a thorn'. Hearing rumours that Catherine had many lovers (some of which were definitely true), he soon changed his mind on that score! He had her executed on 13 February 1542.

Second-hand? Of course the dress isn't second-hand. Where would I get a second-hand wedding dress from?

SCOTCHING THE SCOTS

Throughout these marital 'troubles', there had been unrest in Europe too. Now France and the Holy Roman Empire had fallen out with each other again, Henry thought this would be an excellent time for England to attack France (so long as the Scots – who were ruled by a Roman Catholic king – didn't get involved). Henry flooded the Scottish border with troops, then offered King James V of Scotland a treaty. James refused. The Scots far outnumbered the English forces, but became stuck in the marshes of Solway

Moss. Few were killed, but hundreds of Scots were taken prisoner. King James died soon after – supposedly of shame – and his daughter Mary became Queen of Scots. She was a week old, so not too good at foreign policy.

PROPOSALS TURNED SOUR

On 1 July 1543, it was agreed that a 'treaty of marriage' be made between Henry's son Prince Edward and the baby Queen Mary. This was like an official engagement that would also bring peace . . . and Scotland pretty much under England's control. Now Henry could send 5,000 troops across the Channel to prepare to fight France. With the Scottish problem apparently sorted out, Henry and Charles V united against the French again (surprise, surprise) and planned a massive attack on France in 1544. The Scots then abandoned all its agreements with England and said, 'We're still friends with France really'. The engagement was now OFF and the English spent ten bloody days in Scotland doing some very nasty things to teach them a lesson.

SIXTH AND FINAL WIFE

In the same month that his son Edward was promised the hand of Mary Queen of Scots, July 1543, Henry married for the sixth and final time. His wife was another Catherine: Catherine Parr. (In fact, her name was Catherine Latimer when Henry met her because she had been married twice and outlived both her husbands.) Catherine Parr was kind and caring to all three of her stepchildren. Edward loved her, ten-year-old Elizabeth was obviously very fond of her and even Mary was delighted at how she recognized and accepted her 'royal blood'. Queen Catherine even stood in for King Henry as regent for a bit, while he was over on the continent fighting the French.

A VICTORY OF SORTS

The French town of Boulogne was captured on 18 September 1544. By October, Henry was trying to negotiate peace with the French. So much of the money he'd gained from the dissolution of the monasteries had been spent – some say wasted – on war. His health was really failing him now. He never seemed to be able to shake off a fever, his ulcers were extremely painful and he was carried everywhere. To get his huge hulk upstairs required a winch. By the time he was 55, he'd pretty much given up walking altogether.

MEETING HIS MAKER

Tradition has it that Henry died speaking the name of his third wife, Jane Seymour – the only wife to bear him a son, however sickly. Whether this is true or not, it certainly is true that his last will and testament was to be buried beside Jane in the chapel at Windsor. Henry died at about two o'clock on the morning of Friday 28 January 1547 in St James's Palace. He was holding the hand of Thomas Cranmer, the archbishop who had been with him through thick and thin. He squeezed Cranmer's hand as a sign that he put his trust in Christ. His reign of over thirty-seven years was at an end.

WHAT NEXT?

As you might expect, Henry's son Edward became king after Henry but ill health meant that his reign was a short one. Both of Henry's daughters were to become queen in turn too, but not before the nine-day (yes N-I-N-E D-A-Y) rule of someone called Lady Jane Grey. Roman Catholic Mary had a short but bloody reign whereas Elizabeth's was long and glorious . . . but that's another story, and you can read all about it next.

GET A LIFE!
ELIZABETH I

USEFUL WORDS
(Some more useful than others)

Here are some useful words. Some of them are Elizabethan and some are from the present day. Some appear in this book and others don't . . . except on this page, of course.

Astrologers People who predict the future by studying the stars. (You know, working out horoscopes and all that.)

Duel A private fight, often to the death, between two gentlemen.

Elizabethan Something relating to the period of Elizabeth I's reign. (For example: 'Elizabethan England' means 'England during her time as queen' and 'an Elizabethan playwright' was someone who wroght – sorry, *wrote* – plays during her reign.)

Hedge-creepers Elizabethan robbers who pounced out on their victims from in or behind hedges.

Illegitimate An illegitimate child was a child whose parents weren't married.

Prancer A horse. (A prigger of prancers was a horse thief.)

Regent A person who ruled on behalf of monarch if the monarch was out of the country, too young or too crazy.

YOUNG LIZ

The pink, squidgy baby who was to grow up to be Queen Elizabeth I, one of Britain's most famous monarchs, was born on 7 September 1533. To be more precise, she was born in Greenwich Palace on the south bank of the River Thames. To be even more precise – and, hey, why not? – she was born in Anne Boleyn's bedroom, in Anne Boleyn's bed at around about three o'clock in the afternoon. In case you hadn't worked it out, Anne Boleyn was Elizabeth's mum. She was also King Henry VIII's second wife. (VIII is the Roman numerals for eight. V = 5 and III = 3). It would be nice to say that Anne was most famous for giving birth to such a fantabulous queen-to-be. But that just ain't so. Ms Boleyn is *faaaaar* more famous for having her head chopped off.

SSHH! SECRET SERVICE

Although, or perhaps *because*, Elizabeth's dad-to-be was King of England, Ireland and Wales, he and Anne Boleyn got married in secret on 25 January 1533. Very few people knew about the wedding. It took place so early in the morning that it was still dark! It wasn't until 12 April that year that Anne Boleyn appeared at her first official function as Queen.

RIGHT ROYAL MESS

One reason for the secrecy of the marriage was the mess caused by Henry divorcing his first wife, Catherine of Aragon (not to be confused with the herb tarragon). In those days, England was still a Catholic country and all religious matters came under the control of the Pope. Divorces weren't allowed, so Henry had argued with the Pope that his marriage to Aragon (the queen, not the herb) should be annulled. In other words, it should be officially declared that it hadn't been a proper marriage at all. The Pope wouldn't agree to this, which eventually led to Henry breaking England away from Catholicism.

OH BOY! OH BOY!

In those days, for some reason, many men wanted sons and not daughters. The trouble was that Henry VIII *really* wanted sons – or at least one measly son – who could grow up and become king after him. The reason Henry was so keen to have a son was so that the Tudor name could live on. Even if his daughter married, became queen and had children, the children would have their father's – and not the Tudor – name. When his first wife Catherine of Aragon only produced a daughter, Mary, he divorced her. So Henry then married Anne, and hoped for a baby boy . . .

CHEERS AND FEARS

... but, as you now know, Elizabeth was the result. This didn't bother Henry's subjects (and by that I don't mean Maths, French and Geography, but his people: the English). They lit bonfires in celebration and church bells were rung throughout the land, though mainly in churches, of course. Anne Boleyn, on the other hand, was probably more than a little disappointed that she hadn't been able to give Henry, her hubby, the boy so longed for, and was probably frightened too. (Talking of hands, Anne Boleyn had six fingers on one of hers!)

LET DOWN ON ALL SIDES

According to an ambassador's report, one reason why Henry was even more upset was that his 'physicians, astrologers, wizards and witches all ... affirmed it would be a boy' and a letter had even been written in advance that announced the birth of a prince. Now that had to be changed to 'princess'. The ambassador cheerfully went on to conclude that God had abandoned poor Henry!

THE NAME GAME

Elizabeth was christened in a silver font, underneath a canopy of crimson satin fringed with gold, on Wednesday 10 September. She was just three days old. The princess was wearing purple velvet with a long train edged with ermine (the same fur that edges lords' ceremonial robes). The end of the train was carried by Elizabeth's grandpa – Anne Boleyn's father – Thomas Boleyn, Earl of Wiltshire.

For some reason, the original choice of name was going to be 'Mary', the same as her older half-sister. Perhaps Henry thought all young girls looked the same so it would make life easier if his daughters had the same name? Fortunately, they settled for 'Elizabeth' instead.

OUT OF SIGHT

Henry didn't want a baby girl cluttering up the palaces, so he had little Liz sent to live in the country in the old wooden manor house of Hatfield. Anne had to stay put, though, so it was down to one of Elizabeth's great aunts to care for her. Anne Boleyn stayed with the king because he wanted her to have another baby, but a *boy* this time. When Elizabeth was a year old Anne Boleyn did actually get pregnant again, and with a boy. Sadly, he died before he was even born.

STEPMUM ONE, HERE SHE COMES

Henry VIII gave up on Elizabeth's mother after that. In his mind, she'd failed him and, charming chap that he was, he thought that it was all her fault. In the meantime, he'd found a new love-of-his life, a woman called Jane Seymour. But this didn't stop Henry from seeing his daughter Elizabeth. Delighted by the death of his first wife, Catherine, on 8 January 1536, Henry even had Elizabeth delivered to his Hampton Court palace to take part in the 'celebrations'. He had Elizabeth brought into church to a proud blast of trumpets, and he later carried her around in his arms to show her off like a proud dad. Perhaps this was partly to show how important she was compared to Mary, his other daughter born of his disgraced, now dead, ex-wife.

GOING, GOING, GONE

Things didn't go so well for Elizabeth's mum. Henry started spreading rumours that poor old Anne Boleyn had been going out with other men when he wasn't looking. Because he was king and she was queen, this was a very serious matter. Anne was put on trial and found guilty of the charges. As a result, Henry could – and did – have their marriage annulled. Two days later, on 19 May 1536, she was beheaded at the Tower of London. (Beheaded is the polite term for having someone's head chopped off.) People often imagine that the executioner was some huge, burly bloke with a black hood over his head and a great big axe. In truth, this executioner was a very fine French swordsman . . . with a great big sword. So that's all right then.

THE LAST LAUGH

Sir William Kingston, Constable of the Tower of London, was surprised to find that, in the days leading up to her execution, Anne Boleyn seemed to be very cheerful most of the time. She laughed a lot and once joked with him that she'd heard the executioner was 'very good' and that she had a little neck. She then put her hands around her neck 'laughing heartily'. Perhaps it was nerves.

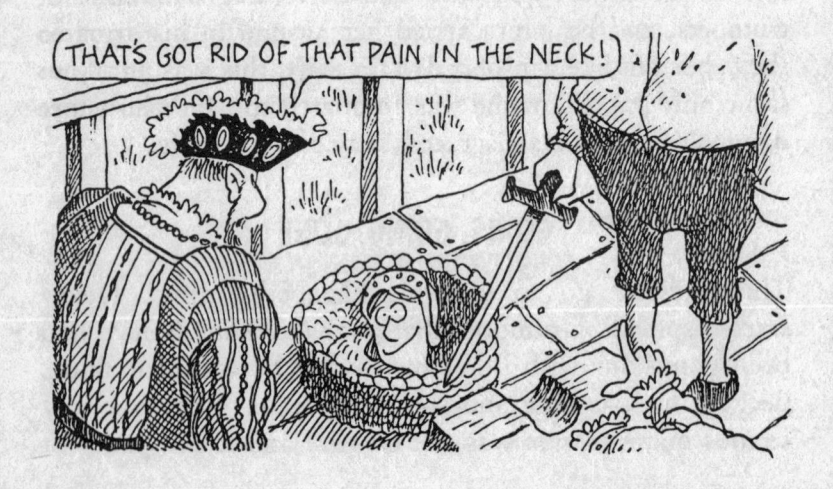

UNPAID BILLS

Although those who cared *for* Elizabeth were many miles from the palace, her mother still cared *about* her very much. Anne Boleyn visited Elizabeth often and, on her death, left a number of unpaid bills for expensive little items she'd ordered for her baby girl. These included caps made of taffeta and satin and even a crimson fringe to go around Elizabeth's cradle.

HEIRS AND FEARS

When Anne Boleyn died, Henry had three living children. His oldest child was, in fact, a boy. He was the Duke of Richmond. The trouble was, because Henry had never been married to Elizabeth Blount, the boy's mother – making the boy illegitimate – the Duke could never become king after him. Then came Catherine of Aragon's daughter, Mary. For a while, she'd been heir to the throne but, when Henry finally managed to divorce her mother, she was declared 'a bastard' and lost that right. Now we come to Elizabeth. With the other two out of the running, she then became 'heir apparent' (the next in line for the throne) . . . until her father had his marriage to *her* mother annulled just before her execution. When that happened, Elizabeth also lost her right to be queen.

OUTGROWN USEFULNESS

Now that Elizabeth was no longer such an important royal, things took a turn for the worse for her, with no more visits from her mother or father. Elizabeth soon grew out of her clothes without having any new ones to wear instead.

Things got so bad that Elizabeth's great aunt, Lady Bryan, had to write to King Henry's right-hand man, Thomas Cromwell, asking him to arrange for her to have some new clothes. This he did, as well as sorting out exactly how Elizabeth should be treated. Though no longer heir apparent, she was then officially recognized as the King's younger daughter and money was spent on her household.

IF YOU DON'T GET SOME NEW CLOTHES SOON, I WANT DANGER MONEY AND A CRASH HELMET!

BOUNCING BABY BROTHER

On 12 October 1537, Henry VIII's third wife, Jane Seymour, gave him what he'd always dreamt of: a legitimate male heir. If there had been bonfires and excitement when Elizabeth had been born, they were nothing compared to the celebrations that now spread throughout the kingdom. More than two thousand guns were fired from the Tower of London. Although only four years old, Elizabeth played an important official role at her half-brother's christening in the chapel at Hampton Court. She carried the christening mantle (or gown) but, because she was so little, she in turn was carried by Jane Seymour's brother Edward! Edward was also the name of the baby prince. Sadly, Jane Seymour died on 24 October, just twelve days after his birth.

STEPMUM NUMBER TWO

Elizabeth was six when her father married again. This, her second stepmother, was Anne of Cleves (not to be confused with cloves), a strict German Protestant. She and Henry just didn't really get along from the word go. So, by the following year, he'd managed to divorce her, throwing in three large houses, their flashy contents, an annual allowance and the rather odd title of 'the King's beloved sister' . . . which everyone knew that she wasn't.

COUSIN CATHERINE

Next, Henry swiftly married the beautiful Catherine Howard. Catherine was Elizabeth's mum's first cousin, which made her Elizabeth's cousin too! Because of this, she showed an interest in little Liz and even gave her an important place at a banquet celebrating her wedding. (The place you sat at an official banquet showed just how important you were, or weren't.) Sadly, Elizabeth's dad soon decided that Catherine, his 'rose without a thorn', wasn't quite the woman he'd imagined her to be. Like cousin Anne before her, Catherine Howard was beheaded at the Tower of London on 13 February 1542. Her headless body was buried next to the headless body of Elizabeth's mother. The poor eight-year-old must have been beginning to wonder what it was about her family that Henry disliked so much! She is said to have sworn then that she would never marry.

THE FINAL STEPMUM

Elizabeth's fourth and final stepmother was Catherine Parr, though her name was Lady Latimer when Henry met her because she had been married twice and outlived both her husbands. Catherine Parr was kind and caring to all three of her stepchildren. (The Duke of Richmond, the fourth – truly illegitimate – stepson had died before Prince Edward was born.) Edward loved her. Ten-year-old Elizabeth found her caring. Even the rather bitter 27-year-old Mary was delighted that the new queen recognized and accepted her 'royal blood'.

ROLE MODEL

Catherine Parr was an excellent role model for Elizabeth. As a woman she was well-educated, witty, clever and graceful. Queen

Catherine even stood in for King Henry as regent for a short time, while he was over on the continent leading the English army against the French. Unlike Elizabeth in later years, though, she had a king to bow down to. Elizabeth would go it alone.

ON THE WRITE TRACK

Elizabeth was educated at home. In the past, it hadn't been thought that it was worth teaching girls how to read and write, but that was before there were printed books. Then, in 1455, a German called Johannes Gutenberg printed the first book and, more importantly in England, William Caxton set up a printing press over here in 1476. Now it was the done thing for all rich girls to be able to read them.

I CAN READ THIS STANDING ON MY HEAD!

WOULDN'T IT BE EASIER TO TURN THE BOOK THE RIGHT WAY UP, M'LADY?

LANGUAGE! LANGUAGE!

It was very important for royals to speak foreign languages – girls too – because, more often than not, they might be married off to foreign royals in marriages of convenience. (In other words, 'You can marry my daughter if you lend us a load of guns and ships to fight a common enemy.') Latin was important because it was the language used by scholars and the Church. (Not the building but the powerful Pope, archbishops and the like.) French was often considered the language of diplomacy. If you insulted someone in French it probably didn't sound as rude as if you said it in English.

As well as English, Latin and French, Princess Elizabeth could also speak Italian fluently. Her Greek and Spanish were said to be quite good, her Flemish (a variety of Dutch which non-French speakers in Flanders spoke) wasn't bad, and she knew more than a few words of Welsh.

BABY BRIDE?

Before the baby Elizabeth was even two years old, and still heir apparent to the throne, it was suggested that she should become engaged to the youngest son of the King of France, the Duke of Angoulême. One condition was that the 14-year-old Duke come over to England to be educated. Fortunately for Elizabeth in later life, the French king wanted the boy educated at home and, when the fuss blew up about Anne Boleyn's trial, he took her side instead of Henry's. The idea of the engagement was over.

HE LOOKS A BIT OLD FOR ME!

MISSED A BEAT

Elizabeth's education was quite unusual in that her tutor, Roger Ascham, didn't beat her. Beating kids was thought to be a very good way of teaching them things. Perhaps Mr Ascham didn't beat her because he thought it cruel. Perhaps he didn't do it in case her father got to hear about it and decided to chop *his* head off.

EXCELLENT REPORTS

By the time that Elizabeth was just six it was said that, even if she never bothered to have another lesson in her life, her knowledge would be a credit to the king. Roger Ascham went even further. He said that Elizabeth's mind 'had no womanly weakness, her perseverance is equal to that of a man.' If someone said that today, it would be taken as an insult, but back then in Tudor times, that was meant as a real compliment. Elizabeth was dead brainy and knowledgeable, and there was no argument about it. Aged eleven, she translated a whole book from the French, bound it in a cover she'd embroidered herself, and gave it to Catherine Parr as a New Year's gift!

During Henry's last years, his son Edward lived with his daughter Elizabeth at Hatfield, and she and her half-brother and sister even had lessons together.

THE ROYAL LINE

In the Act of Succession of 1544, Mary and Elizabeth were officially placed in line to the throne after Edward and any of Henry's children which Catherine Parr might have. In other words they were far further down the pecking order than they had been before, but at least they were back on the list after having been struck off altogether. They were officially back in line to the throne, even if not first in line. They were princesses, not 'ladies', once more.

LIFE AFTER HENRY

Elizabeth's father, Henry VIII, died in January 1547. Her stepbrother, crowned Edward VI, was only nine years old. The real power lay with the Lord Protector Edward Seymour (who had carried Elizabeth at Prince Edward's christening) and Cardinal Thomas Cranmer (who'd been Henry's right-hand man after Cromwell). They proved an unpopular combination and, after it was agreed that a peasants' revolt wasn't dealt with strongly enough, Seymour soon lost power and ended up being hanged.

ELIZABETH AND THE OTHER SEYMOUR

When Henry died, Elizabeth's stepmother, Catherine Parr (now widowed for the third time) married one of the Seymours – Edward's brother Thomas. Being married to the ex-Queen of England must have given Thomas Seymour big ambitions because, when Catherine died, Seymour turned his attention to Elizabeth. Soon rumours were flying about that they would marry next. It never happened. He was sent to the Tower of London along with two other members of Elizabeth's household, now back in Hatfield.

Then rumours started that Elizabeth was pregnant with his child. She knew the importance of public opinion – of what ordinary men and women felt – so asked to visit the new king, to show that she had nothing to hide. This request was refused.

THE SICKLY KING

Edward had always been a sickly prince and, as king, he got no better. When he misbehaved or did badly in lessons – just because he was king now didn't mean his education ground to a halt – *he* wasn't the one to be beaten or whipped . . . it was someone else's job to stand in for him: the whipping boy's! Then Edward caught tuberculosis. He started coughing up blood. Soon he'd given up eating, was covered in sores, his hair was falling out and so were his fingernails and toenails. He died on 6 July 1553. Elizabeth had just moved up one place in line for the throne.

NO, NOT MARY YET

With Edward dead and Catherine Parr having had no children with Henry, you might expect that Mary was the next to be crowned. WRONG. Act of Succession or no Act of Succession, the Protestants who were now the real power behind the throne saw Mary as a dreaded C-A-T-H-O-L-I-C. (Remember, Henry had been a fully fledged Catholic before he broke away from the Pope and 'The Church of England' was born.) They chose the granddaughter of Henry's sister to be queen instead! Called Lady Jane Grey, she was forced into the role.

NINE-DAY WONDER

Queen Jane was on the throne for exactly nine days – yes, you read that right the first time, nine *days* – before Mary's supporters swept Mary into power. You can probably guess what happened to Jane in 1554, even though she was only sixteen. Yup, off with her head.

BLOODY MARY

So now Elizabeth's older half-sister was on the throne at last. If she died, then Elizabeth could end up queen if she wasn't careful, so Mary thought it important to marry and have kids. The man she chose to marry had a brilliant name (Philip) but was a Catholic and King of Spain, which didn't make him a wildly popular choice with her subjects. Another thing which made Mary unpopular was that she was very strict about heresy. In her father's almost 38-year reign he had 81 people put to death for heresy. In Mary's five-year reign she had 280 put to death. That's an average of 56 people a year instead of Henry's 2.13 . . . though how you put 0.13 of a heretic to death without hurting the remaining 0.87 of him/her, is another matter! Anyway, you can see how she earned the nickname Bloody Mary.

ELIZABETH MEETS MARY

Mary (now Queen) and Elizabeth (now heir apparent) met at Aldgate and entered London with Elizabeth in place of honour behind the new queen. After which, Elizabeth spent much of her time in Mary's court... The trouble was that Elizabeth didn't want to be seen to be too strongly connected with unpopular Catholicism, and Mary, in turn, was suspicious of her much younger, and apparently more popular half-sister! In 1554 these matters were resolved. Elizabeth was accused of plotting against Bloody Mary and was sent to the Tower!

PRISONER!

It must have been a frightening time for Elizabeth. Her mother had been beheaded at the Tower. Her cousin Catherine Howard had been beheaded at the Tower... and now here she was. She didn't get special treatment either – her cell was opposite the passageway leading to the loos. A few months later however, on 19 May 1554, Elizabeth was taken to Oxfordshire and the rather tatty palace of Woodstock. She was still a prisoner, but away from that dreadful place. Mary wanted to marry her off to some foreigner who would take her abroad and out of the way!

LOSING HOPE

Elizabeth's future looked far from sunny. To make her own right to the throne watertight, Mary had passed an act saying that her father's divorce from her mother Catherine of Aragon had been illegal. The knock-on effect of this was that Henry's marriage to Elizabeth's mum, Anne Boleyn, was even more bogus and that Elizabeth was even more illegitimate (if such a thing were possible)! Then Mary appeared to get pregnant, and Elizabeth's chances of ever becoming queen looked very slim. As it turned out, Mary was only imagining things. She never had a child. In 1556, now back in Hatfield and amongst old friends, Elizabeth once again made it clear that she wouldn't marry, whatever anyone else might want.

BYE-BYE, BLOODY MARY

Mary managed to make herself even more unpopular with her subjects (the English, Irish and Welsh, but not the Scots who had their own monarch). Over on the Continent, her forces lost the town of Calais to the French, which had been under English control for 200 years. 'When I am dead and opened, you shall find Calais written on my heart,' she said, realizing the seriousness of the loss. She died of cancer on 17 November 1558. News soon reached the 25-year-old Elizabeth that, despite everything, she was now Queen of England!

GOOD QUEEN BESS

When Elizabeth became Queen of England, she wasn't known as Queen Elizabeth the First, because no one knew that there would be a Queen Elizabeth the Second coming to the throne in 1952. She was simply Queen Elizabeth. Later, she was given other nicknames, including 'Gloriana' and 'Good Queen Bess' . . . but not all to her face. It was safer to call her 'Your Gracious Majesty' or something equally grovelling.

PUBLIC DUTY

From the word go, Elizabeth knew how important it was to get the people on her side. When she rode into London on 14 January 1559, the day before her coronation, she made a point of waving and smiling at the huge crowds of people who had come out onto the streets to greet her – instead of looking stuck-up and haughty like many kings and queens had done before her.

PUBLIC FACE - THE MASK OF BEAUTY

Today, we'd describe Elizabeth as being brilliant at 'public relations'. In the days long before photographs, film and television, she found a way of controlling how people saw her. She created something called 'the mask of beauty'. It was a template – a strict pattern – which every single artist had to follow when drawing a picture or painting a portrait of her. In this way, she could be sure that she appeared the same in every portrait, so people would think that this was what she really looked like . . . and that look was 'beautiful'.

DEE TIME

Elizabeth chose to have her coronation on 15 January 1559 because that was the date recommended to her by the famous scientist Dr John Dee. He wasn't what we'd call a scientist today. For a start, he never wore a white lab coat but usually dressed in black. Not only that, he also dabbled in magic and astrology. His assistant Kelly claimed to see things in a crystal ball which he would tell Dr Dee about. Dee would then work out their meaning . . . and this is how he came up with the lucky date for the coronation.

CORONATION CAPERS

If this was a lucky date for the coronation, it's hard to imagine what it'd have been like on an *unlucky* one. The crowds of well-wishers were so excited to be present at such an important and joyful occasion – Bloody Mary having been so unpopular with most of them – that they decided they wanted souvenirs to remember the day by. There was a beautiful blue (not red, don't believe everything you read) carpet which had been laid out for the Queen to walk from Westminster Hall to the Abbey. Someone had the smart idea of cutting out a tiny piece of carpet to keep. After all, who would notice such a small hole? No one. But once *loads* of people had cut out pieces, the holes became bigger, and there were lots of them! Elizabeth proved to be very good at dodging them but the poor old Duchess of Norfolk, who was holding the end of the Queen's train, kept tripping and stumbling over them.

MARRIED TO HER COUNTRY

By now it was beginning to dawn on her courtiers that when she *said* she wasn't going to marry, she *meant* she wasn't going to marry. This was amazing for two main reasons.

Firstly, because she was a woman and shouldn't women have a man to tell them what to do? (Don't punch me, I'm only explaining the feelings at the time!) Secondly, if she didn't marry she couldn't have any children to become her heirs to the crown. And surely she wanted heirs? Didn't *all* kings and queens want heirs? This was incredible! A free-thinking woman more interested in ruling for the here-and-now, than having kids for the later-on! Elizabeth explained that she was 'married to England', and gained a new nickname: The Virgin Queen.

MERRIE ENGLAND

After the harsh years of half-sister Mary's rule, England seemed a far more merry place under Elizabeth – 'merry' was often spelled 'merrie' back then, but not always (because spelling didn't seem that important). Although still a part of Tudor Times, life during Elizabeth's reign later became known as the Elizabethan Age. It was the age of great writers such as William Shakespeare (I bet you've heard of him), Christopher Marlowe, Edmund Spenser, Philip Sidney and Ben Jonson. You can read about some famous Elizabethans on pages 113 and 114.

JUST AS SOON AS I'VE DECIDED HOW TO SPELL 'SHAKESPEARE', I CAN START WRITING SOME PLAYS!

ACT OF SUPREMACY

When Bloody Mary had been queen, she'd given control of the Church back to the Pope, as it had been before Henry VIII's reforms. Now that Elizabeth was in charge, she passed a law called the Act of Supremacy. This put the nation's Church under the control of the monarch (in other words, *her*), and royal officials, judges, clergymen and the like had to swear an oath of loyalty to her, or lose their jobs.

SCOTLAND OR GROTLAND?

The Scots' queen was Mary Stuart, the young wife of Francis, heir to the throne of France. She was also Elizabeth's cousin. Mary Stuart lived in France with Francis, who later became king but, when he died in 1560, she returned to Scotland. Mary is said to have been very tall and beautiful while Scotland was thought by many non-Scots to be a real hellhole . . . and that's putting it politely. Mary Stuart didn't like the bad weather. She spoke French and most Scots didn't, and whilst she was a Catholic, most Scottish people were Puritans – extreme Protestants – but she was still their queen.

PURE PURITAN VIEWS

A Puritan organization in Scotland, called the Congregation, was very powerful. It encouraged a pure, simple approach to Christianity without what it saw as unnecessary trappings. Puritans were against statues and paintings in churches, and against rituals such as wearing wedding rings, and making the sign of the cross. They didn't want people wearing colourful clothes either, and dancing was certainly a no-no.

A WORRY TO ELIZABETH

Having cousin Mary up in Scotland was a worry to Elizabeth. Like Mary, most of Europe was Catholic, so against Elizabeth and England, while – just across the border – was this beautiful, young, Catholic queen.

Many people in Scotland wanted Elizabeth to marry the Earl of Arran and claim the crown of Scotland. A Protestant Queen of England as ruler of Scotland seemed, to many, a better choice than a French-speaking Catholic . . . but Elizabeth had no intention of marrying anyone. She refused the Earl's proposal twice, and the Scottish people felt they were being abandoned.

A CLAIM TO THE ENGLISH THRONE

As Elizabeth's cousin, Mary Queen of Scots wanted to be officially made 'heir presumptive' to the English throne. In other words, she would instantly be 'second in the kingdom' and become Queen of England when Elizabeth died, if

Elizabeth didn't marry and have kids. Elizabeth said that she was worried that if she agreed to this, Mary would become the centre of attention for plots to overthrow her and put Mary in her place. The good thing for Elizabeth was that, if Mary wanted to become Queen of England after her, she might have some influence over her cousin.

MR MARY

When it came to Mary Queen of Scots choosing a new husband, it was time for Elizabeth to use any influence she had. Mary was seen as a very good 'catch'. Already Queen of Scots and, possibly, to be Queen of England, plenty of important and powerful men wanted to be her husband. Elizabeth was particularly worried that if cousin Mary married someone from the royal families of Austria, Spain or France, she could end up with a power-hungry Catholic king right on her border.

Elizabeth decided to unleash her secret weapon on Mary: Lord Dudley. Lord Dudley was Elizabeth's favourite, a dashing courtier and a bit of a smoothy too. Some historians believed that he and Elizabeth had even been in love with each other, for a while. Whether Dudley rejected Mary or Mary rejected Dudley we're not sure, but Elizabeth would have to come up with another match . . .

DEADLY DARNLEY

The man Mary did marry was another Lord, called Darnley. He was a real silver-tongued talker and a good-looker and was despised by the Scottish lords. Once they'd got married, Mary found a new side to Lord Darnley – a nasty, rude side which made her cry. He was a drunken brute, and Mary turned to her secretary, David Rizzio, for a shoulder to cry on. Darnley thought they were doing a lot more than that together so he arranged to have Rizzio stabbed fifty times right before Mary's eyes.

MORE MURDER

In February 1567 Darnley himself came to an even more bizarre end. Ill and in bed in Edinburgh one night, he didn't live to see the dawn. In the early hours of the morning there was a huge explosion and his body went flying out of the bed, through the Edinburgh skies and landed with a squelch. Someone had blown up the house he was staying in! That won't have bothered Darnley, though. He'd been strangled before the gunpowder had even been set alight! Soon everyone knew that a man called Lord Bothwell had arranged the dirty deed and, rumour had it, he'd done it for Mary.

MARRIAGE 3 – THE SEQUEL

No sooner was Darnley dead than Mary was forced into marrying Lord Bothwell . . . but he fled the country when his enemies came after him. Mary was then locked up in a castle on an island in the middle of Lochleven (a loch or 'big lake').

INTO THE ARMS OF THE ENEMY

Mary managed to escape by boat, having disguised herself as a serving woman. (This sort of disguise crops up a number of times in Scottish history and it's not always a woman under that thick skirt and tatty shawl.) Powerless and friendless in Scotland, Mary abdicated and fled to England to 'throw herself on the mercy of the Queen'. This meant saying something along the lines of, 'Look, sorry if we haven't always seen eye-to-eye, but will you be nice to me? I promise to be good.' But Elizabeth refused to see her. Mary left behind her infant son James, who became Scotland's king.

STOP THOSE PLOTS!

Elizabeth let Mary stay in England – even if it was under guard and in the north, away from court – and, exactly as she'd predicted, many Catholics wanted to see her on the throne and took the opportunity to plot against Elizabeth. In 1583, Francis Throckmorton planned an invasion of England by Catholic Spain. He was caught, tortured and gave away the names of his co-conspirators. The invasion was over before it began.

An Italian banker called Roberto Ridolfi had also planned invasion in 1571 but his plot was uncovered by Elizabeth's secret service. Although Ridolfi himself was out of the country, so avoided arrest, the other plotters weren't so lucky.

OVER A BARREL

Of course, Mary herself could deny having anything to do with these plots. She could claim that they were nothing to do with her. She hadn't *asked* Throckmorton and Ridolfi to arrange these Catholic invasions. When it came to the Babington Plot, though, Elizabeth had her over a barrel. Babington wasn't planning an invasion, he simply wanted to assassinate Elizabeth and put Mary Stuart on the throne.

Elizabeth's secret service found out about the plot and Mary's own involvement in 1586 when they discovered coded messages between Mary and the plotters, kept in waterproof leather pouches, hidden inside barrels of beer.

GUILTY!

Elizabeth was shocked and dismayed when she heard the news. Not only had her cousin betrayed her but, if found guilty, Elizabeth would have to sign her death warrant. You couldn't have people guilty of plots to murder the Queen of England getting off scot-free. (*Scot*-free . . . Mary Queen of *Scots*. Geddit? Never mind.) Mary was tried at Fotheringhay Castle in Northamptonshire and, indeed, found guilty. After much soul-searching, Elizabeth signed the death warrant but did not pass it on to her ministers. Finally, they decided that they had to take action on their own.

COUSIN MARY GETS THE CHOP

On 8 February 1587, Mary Stuart was executed in the great hall at Fotheringhay Castle. The night before, she'd written letters to friends and given instructions as

*PERHAPS THEY SHOULD HAVE CALLED **THIS** MARY 'BLOODY MARY.'*

to who should have which pieces of her jewellery once she'd gone. Dressed in a black satin dress, it took two or three hacks of the axe to separate her head from her neck. Even then, the lips on her severed head are said to have moved for about a quarter of an hour, as if in silent prayer. Mary's head had rolled across the floor and the executioner picked it up by what he thought was her hair. It turned out to be a brown wig. Underneath it, Mary's real hair was grey . . . while underneath Mary's petticoat was her terrified tiny pet dog!

THE QUEEN'S FURY

Elizabeth was said to have been furious when she found out that her ministers had taken matters into their own hands. She openly grieved whilst the rest of the county rejoiced. Remembering what we said about Elizabeth being good at public relations, it is, of course, possible that she was putting on an act of sadness so that the Catholic countries wouldn't be so quick to blame and condemn her.

JIM LAD

Mary's son James, already King of Scotland, was so eager to become King of England when Elizabeth eventually died that he wanted to be on friendly terms with her. Suddenly, the situation between Scotland and England got a lot better.

THE SPANISH ARMADA

When Elizabeth came to the throne, England's coffers were almost empty, meaning that there was very little money in the royal purse. One advantage of England now being Protestant was that some Protestants on the Continent, persecuted by their Catholic rulers, came over to this country ... bringing their skills and knowledge with them. These included everything from glass-making and silk-weaving to mining and metalworking. Soon England began to make money in trade.

WOOLLY SUBJECTS

England's biggest seller abroad was wool, and that meant that the English and Welsh countryside was covered with sheep. Some people owned just one small flock but a rich nobleman might own as many as 17,000 animals. During the Elizabethan Age there were about three times as many sheep as people! Elizabeth passed a law making people wear sheep's wool hats on Sundays. This meant more money for the wool traders, and more money from them in taxes to *her*!

RULE THE WAVES?

Being an island nation, England needed ships to trade goods. There was no shortage of intrepid sailors and explorers in Elizabeth's reign. Probably the two most famous of these are Sir Francis Drake and Sir Walter Raleigh.

THE GREAT SPUD SAGA

(Nearly) everyone knows the famous story of Sir Walter Raleigh introducing Queen Elizabeth, and England, to that now-familiar vegetable the potato, which she loved. The only problem with this story is that *he* didn't and *she* didn't.

Sir Walter didn't introduce the potato to Britain. Most people who worry about such things seem to think it was brought back by a mathematician called Thomas Harriot (not to be confused with the haricot bean).

It's said that Good Queen Bess didn't get to enjoy the potato because no one knew how to cook it. A group of nobles ate the leaves and stems (which are poisonous) and threw away the actual potato part . . . They ended up so ill that no one else in Britain bothered tackling a tatty for about another hundred years!

SIR WALTER RALEIGH

It was true, however, that Sir Walter was one of the queen's favourites. Pointy beards were all the rage (for men) and Sir Walter's was one of the pointiest. He also wore a large ruff – a big frilly collar, fashionable with men and women. As well having a pointy beard and big ruff, Sir Walter Raleigh (pronounced to rhyme with 'poorly' rather than 'pally') tried to set up a colony in America, to make trade easier. He chose the place and called it Virginia after the *Virgin* Queen.

TO THE COLONY!

It was all very well choosing the spot, but Sir Walter wasn't the one who actually had to live there. He was too busy off doing other flashy things. Seven-ships'-worth of colonists set off for Virginia in 1585. By 1586, seven-ships'-worth of colonists were asking to come home. Life out there was tough.

Sir Walter tried setting up the colony again in 1587, but that also met with failure.

UP IN SMOKE

Potato or no potato, it was Sir Walter who made smoking tobacco the in-thing in England. You might have thought that smokers guessed it was bad for them because they coughed up black tar, but that was the very reason why they thought it was *good* for them! (It's a funny Olde Worlde, eh?) They assumed that everyone – smokers and non smokers alike – were filled with this evil stuff, and that smoking tobacco helped you cough it up. How wrong they were.

UNACCEPTABLE FAILURE

Later in life, Sir Walter led an English expedition to try to find the fabulous South American gold of the legendary El Dorado . . . He failed and when he returned to England, Elizabeth's successor (Cousin Mary Stuart Queen of Scots' son James) had him beheaded.

A HARD LIFE ON THE OCEAN WAVE

Life on the ocean wave could be as tough as old boots. There are actual reports of sailors cutting up their boots, boiling the leather and eating them . . . but that was only after they'd eaten all the spare candles and any rats unlucky enough to be caught. Rations were scarce and disease was very common. Far more sailors died from illness than in battle, with malaria and yellow fever spreading through ships like wild fire (which is like tame fire, only angrier).

The real killer, though, was scurvy (a lack of vitamin C). If only they'd known that a diet of fresh fruit would have helped cure that.

ARISE, SIR PIRATE

About the only Elizabethan seafarer as famous as Sir Walter was Sir Francis Drake. Sir Francis Drake hadn't been born a 'Sir'. He was knighted for attacking passing Spanish ships and stealing masses and masses of gold from them ... oh, and for sailing round the world between 1577 and 1580. He was knighted at a ceremony on board his ship the *Golden Hind*. Elizabeth's garter slid down her leg as she boarded, much to the delight of a goggle-eyed French envoy. England was, of course, totally against piracy ... unless it was the crews of official English ships who were the ones behaving like pirates. In this trip alone, Sir Francis Drake brought back about treasure worth about £600,000. That's still a lot of money today, but back then it was an absolute fortune and he gave by far the most of it to Elizabeth.

BOWLS!

Sir Francis Drake is famous for playing bowls. I don't mean he had shelves of bowls trophies, I mean that he was famous for being interrupted during a game of bowls to be told that the Spanish Armada was coming. An armada is nothing more than a fleet of ships, but the Spanish Armada is one of the most famous in history.

TROUBLE BREWS

In case you hadn't guessed already, England and Spain were sworn enemies. King Philip (good name) of Spain was the ruler of the largest and most successful Catholic empire in the world. Queen Elizabeth was the ruler of the now-prosperous Protestant England. She supported the Protestant Dutch in their war against Spain and her nippy little English ships were doing a good job of piracy in Spanish waters. Elizabeth and England had become more than a thorn in Philip's side.

THE ARMADA IS PLANNED

The plan was a straightforward one. A huge Spanish Armada of a great many *big* ships would zoom down the English Channel, destroying any English resistance. It would then reach the Netherlands, defeat the Protestant

Dutch rebels, join forces with the Spaniards already over there, then come back and invade England. It should all be over by teatime ... That was the plan, anyway.

BIG GUNS

The Spanish Armada was made up of 130 ships with 30,000 men, 19,000 of whom were soldiers. They had 2,431 guns and 125,790 cannonballs to fire at the English and Dutch. The guns could only be fired with any accuracy at distances of less than 200 metres (especially when a ship was rolling in the waves). There had to be a break of five minutes before firing a gun again, or it could get red hot and even explode.

NICE ONE, CHARLIE

Like Sir Walter Raleigh and the potato, many people think that Sir Francis Drake led the English fleet against the Armada. Wrong again! That honour belongs to the English Lord High Admiral, Charles Howard. Despite the impressive seafaring title, he wasn't really a sailor. He divided the defending fleet into four squadrons – led by himself, Drake (now the Vice-Admiral), Martin Frobisher (who had sailed to some very cold parts of the world and even kidnapped an Inuit), and a man named John Hawkins.

HAPLESS HAWKINS

In 1567, Sir John Hawkins had set sail from Plymouth with six ships. His flagship was called the *Jesus of Lubeck* which may sound grand, but kept taking in water (which is sailor-speak for 'it leaked like crazy'). After helping out an African king along the coast of West Africa, Sir John and his crew then sailed on to South America. During a storm in the Caribbean, the *Jesus of Lubeck* started falling to pieces, which came as no surprise to anyone. What was amazing was that it had lasted that long! While waiting for repairs, the Spanish showed up, but Hawkins was friendly and let them into port next to his fleet . . . which was very foolish. That night, the Spanish attacked. They didn't like Protestant English ships trading in what the Spanish saw as their territory. Now the Armada was coming, here was Hawkins' chance for revenge.

SINGEING THE KING OF SPAIN'S BEARD

The attack was far from a surprise. Once again, Elizabeth's secret service was brilliant. English spies sent back full reports of Spanish preparations, whereas security was so tight in English ports that a stranger had little chance of getting near them. On 12 April 1587, Drake was given the job of making life as difficult as possible for the Spanish assembling their forces. He left Portsmouth and sailed into the port of Cadiz, destroying a large number of defenceless Spanish ships still being prepared for war! He even took control of six Spanish galleons and brought them back as prizes. As well as ships, he'd also destroyed stores and provisions and set back the Armada by at least a year!

ELIZABETH MEETS THE TROOPS

When the long-awaited attack came, it's important to remember that King Philip wasn't expecting a big sea battle. He intended to knock out England's 'inferior' fleet, then come back and invade the country with Spanish troops he planned to pick up from the Netherlands later. This plan was so well known that, as the Armada sailed up the English Channel in July 1588, Elizabeth sailed down the River Thames to meet up with the English army at Tilbury. She was dressed in white, from the white feather in her steel helmet to her shoes. Even her horse was white and she carried a silver baton. She must have been an amazing sight.

As it was, she didn't need to lead her army into battle. News reached her while she was still at Tilbury that the Spanish Armada had been defeated and what ships remained had fled into the North Sea!

SPEECH! SPEECH!

Elizabeth's speech at Tilbury is a very famous one. She told her troops: 'I know I have but the body of a weak and feeble woman, but I have the heart and stomach of a king, and a king of England too!' If, by 'stomach' she meant the stomach for a fight, no one who knew her would argue with that. You can read on page 107 how she boxed the Earl of Essex around the ears, and she often punched, kicked or threw things at her secretaries. Come to think of it, that body of hers can't have been that 'feeble' now, can it?

ARMADA ATTACK!

Both the size of the English fleet and the size of its actual ships were smaller than the Spanish. What British ships lacked in number they made up for in manoeuvrability. They could move more quickly and turn around more easily in the cramped conditions of a ten-day fight in the English Channel. Yes, this was *ten days* of almost continuous fighting. The world had never seen anything like it. The English Lord High Admiral used many tricks, including sending six flaming ships into the wall of Spanish galleons, setting them ablaze. He also ordered his men to bombard the enemy with gunfire without any attempt to board the Spanish ships, which was unheard of. Why bother to risk men trying to climb aboard a ship when you could simply destroy it? Finally, the English were victorious!

DUTCH DELIGHT!

The Protestant Dutch were so delighted by England's defeat of the Spanish that they struck a special medal to mark the victory. Based on the famous words of the Roman Julius Caesar: 'I came, I saw, I conquered', they showed a picture of the Spanish Armada with the words: 'She came, she saw, she fled' written underneath!

LIMPING HOME

Defeated and downhearted, what was left of the Spanish Armada made its way home, sailing in a loop all the way up the east of England and then around Scotland and Ireland. Meeting with storms and disease, the Armada arrived back in Spain with half the ships it had set out with. Queen Elizabeth's fleet lost none.

ELIZABETH, ESSEX AND THE LATER YEARS

Although Elizabeth never married – and, at one time, even King Philip of Spain had been suggested as a possible husband – she certainly liked dashing men and had her obvious favourites. A number of times this caused a near scandal (which is like a scandal but not quite one). Take the earlier time when there were rumours that she and Lord Dudley were in love. Dudley's wife was found dead at the bottom of the stairs, leaving him free to marry the Queen if she asked him! There's no proof that Dudley had pushed her, perhaps she fell . . . but you can see why tongues started wagging. As it was, he ended up marrying a woman called Lettice (not to be confused with the vegetable – er – lettuce). Elizabeth gave the poor woman the charming nickname 'She-wolf'!

ENTER ESSEX

In later years, Elizabeth's favourite was Essex. If you think that sounds more like a place name than a man's name, you'd be right. His name was actually Robert Devereux. 'Essex' was part of his title, Earl of Essex, but people often call him 'Essex' for short. He became favourite when Lord Dudley died not long after the defeat of the Armada.

EYE CATCHER

It's hardly surprising that the young man caught the Queen's eye. He is said to have been very tall for those days when, for some reason, the average person was a lot smaller than the average person today, striding about the place, leaning forward 'like the neck of a giraffe'! He also had thick, curly hair and sparkling black eyes. It wasn't long before Elizabeth had him at her side most of the time.

RIVALS!

Essex soon got jealous if he thought the Queen was showing the slightest interest in someone else. Once, the Queen watched another young man, called Sir Charles Blount, perform brilliantly in a joust. As a reward, she sent him a golden chess piece – the queen. When Essex heard this, he was furious and called Blount a fool . . . only to be challenged to a duel by him. As a result, Essex was wounded but, rather than feeling sorry for him, Elizabeth thought it was fitting that someone 'should take him down and teach him better manners'. But Essex was soon in trouble again, this time challenging Sir Walter Raleigh over some petty matter.

NEED AND GREED

Elizabeth obviously felt the need to be admired, and Essex was greedy for power, so the pair were good for each other. But Essex was reckless – he often did things without thinking and disliked authority. Once, he tried to join Drake on an expedition when the Queen had already told him he couldn't go! She called him back and gave him a right earful, but soon forgave him. Another time he handed out knighthoods to a group of his friends without asking Elizabeth's permission first!

A RAGE TOO FAR

However attracted she was by Essex's wit and charm, Elizabeth also recognized that he might, one day, play an important part in serving England. He was given a number of different posts including Master of the Horse and Master of the Ordnance . . . but he went too far. A new Lord Deputy needed to be appointed for Ireland and Essex recommended one of his enemies for the job. The reason why was obvious. The Lord Deputy of Ireland would have to live in Ireland so would be out of Essex's way!

When Elizabeth refused, Essex turned his back on her. This was a terrible insult to a monarch, so she hit him round the ears! Essex exploded in a fit of terrible rage and lost control. All male courtiers wore swords, and he grabbed his.

This was crazy! No one behaved like that towards their monarch and got away with it.

... BACK WITH BESS

Essex's enemies were delighted. At best, surely, Elizabeth would have him beheaded or banished? At worst, at least the Queen would no longer favour this headstrong young man who'd grown far too big for his boots. Wrong again. After a very short time of disgrace, Essex was back. In 1599 he was Elizabeth's army commander in Ireland – a position he loved because he'd always wanted to be a great soldier.

THE TROUBLED ISLE

Although Elizabeth was Queen of Ireland and Wales as well as England, Ireland was a particular worry to her for a particular reason. The Irish were Catholics . . . and there was a constant fear that the Spanish would help cause an uprising over there. It was thought that one way around this problem was to fill the country with Protestants, so colonies of Protestant English were 'planted' there.

CRUEL RULE

Not surprisingly, the Irish didn't like these people coming over from England and taking their land. Matters weren't helped by the fact that many English officials, such as the governor of Connaught, treated the Irish more like animals than people – and badly treated animals at that. Soon, the Irish rebelled and, led by the Earl of Tyrone, defeated English troops at Yellow Ford in County Armagh. The

Spanish had planned to send a new Armada, this time to help the Irish, but bad weather forced them back. They didn't seem to have much luck with their armadas!

The English still had control of Dublin and the surrounding land, known as the Pale, and it was to Dublin that Essex brought his army.

DEFEAT AND DISEASE

Essex commanded an army of 1,300 on horseback and 16,000 foot soldiers, and leading them beyond the Pale, he confronted the Irish. Many of his troops were poorly trained, poorly equipped and had barely enough to eat. Soon, many fell ill. He failed to defeat the rebels or to win any glorious victories. This news didn't please Elizabeth back home so, in a last-ditch attempt to stay her favourite, he hurried back to England without even waiting for permission.

BEHIND THE MASK OF BEAUTY

Reaching Nonsuch Palace, without stopping to change his clothes after his long ride across country, Essex burst into Elizabeth's bedroom unannounced. He was still in his muddy boots. This must have been a terrible shock for the Queen.

What must have been a terrible shock for Essex was to see the Queen without wig, without piles of make-up, without her big ruff and sparkling jewels. Here was a balding, grey-haired 66-year-old woman! Amazingly, Elizabeth didn't explode with rage, though she had every right to. As well as invading her bedroom, Essex had also deserted his post in Ireland!

THE EX-EARL OF ESSEX

Again, Essex escaped with his life. Banished from the court, this time he openly turned against Elizabeth. It was *power* he wanted, not her. He sucked up to King James of Scotland and hatched a plot for an English rebellion. In February 1601, he and a few followers began marching on London, trying to whip up support along the way. But no one wanted to be in their gang, so the rebellion failed. Captured in his own home, Elizabeth finally had Essex beheaded on 25 February. His headless body was buried close to that of Elizabeth's mother, Anne Boleyn, which had lain there for almost 65 years.

SAD AND ALONE

As Elizabeth neared the end of her life, she must have been a strange sight. She stopped hiding her baldness under her bright red wigs, had no eyebrows, few teeth and her skin had been ruined by all those years of wearing dangerous lead-based make-up. But she did have the advantage of stunning (if rather strange) clothes, with over 3,000 dresses to choose from.

With Essex dead, she had no real favourite and was depressed and grumpy, convinced that people were plotting to kill her. She'd go about muttering to herself and stabbing curtains with a sword, just in case assassins were hiding behind them waiting to leap out at her!

THE FAMOUS FART

No book about Good Queen Bess would be complete without the famous fart story, and here is as good a place to put it as anywhere. Once, when a courtier was bowing to her before leaving her presence he broke wind. He was so embarrassed that he stayed away from court for seven long years. When he finally returned, he wondered if the Queen would recognize him, or how she would treat him. She took one look at him and laughed. 'Lord,' she said. 'I had forgot the fart!'

FAREWELL, VIRGIN QUEEN

In 1603, aged sixty-nine, the already weak Elizabeth got an ulcer in the throat and became seriously ill. She sat in her room for four days in almost complete silence, then was carried to her bed. Knowing that the Queen was dying, she had been asked who should have the throne of England after her. She is said to have replied: 'Who but my kinsman, the King of Scots?'

On 24 March, she died. The Elizabethan Age and Tudor Times were at an end. Sir Robert Carey rode to Holyrood Castle in Edinburgh to tell King James of Scotland that he was now King James of England too. England had lost its Virgin Queen.

OTHER FAMOUS ELIZABETHANS
(ALMOST IN ALPHABETICAL ORDER, BUT NOT QUITE.)

(c. is short for 'circa', meaning 'about/roughly')

Sir Francis BACON (1561–1626) Philosopher, writer and statesman. In 1785, it was suggested that all of so-called *Shakespeare*'s works were really written by Bacon! Nowadays, most brainy scholars don't think that's true.

William CECIL (1520–98) One of the most – if not *the* most – important men in the whole of England. Much liked by Elizabeth, he was her principal Secretary of State.

Robert CECIL (c.1563–1612) *William Cecil*'s seemingly serious son, who took over his dad's job when he retired. He appeared to be a dignified sort of chap, but loved gambling and parties, and his pet parrot too.

Sir Richard GRENVILLE (c.1541–91) Sir Walter Raleigh's cousin, famous for fighting against fifteen Spanish ships for fifteen hours with his one ship, the *Revenge*. Ordered his crew to blow up the *Revenge* rather than surrender . . . but they surrendered anyway. Sir Richard died of his wounds.

Ben JONSON (1572–1637) Soldier, poet, actor and – possibly – murderer. He got off on a technicality. Might have been a spy for the secret service. We don't know for sure. It's a secret.

Christopher MARLOWE (1564–93) A playwright who was also a member of the secret service. Supposedly stabbed to death in a pub brawl in Deptford. Some believe his death was faked for top secret reasons. (Sssh!) This is all very exciting, isn't it?

William SHAKESPEARE (1564–1616) The most famous writer in the whole world ever, *ever*, which can't be bad. He wrote poems but is probably most famous for his plays, originally performed at the Globe Theatre, London – watched by up to 3,000 people at a time!

Thomas TALLIS (c.1505–85) A famous composer, mainly of church music. Was given the title of 'gentleman of the royal chapel'. Elizabeth loved music, but particularly dancing.

Sir Francis WALSINGHAM (c.1532–90) The head of Elizabeth's highly successful secret service, keeping her up to date with plots and plans at home and abroad.

GET A LIFE!
MARY QUEEN OF SCOTS

USEFUL WORDS
(40% of which begin with the letter 'R')

Calvinist A follower of the teachings of John Calvin, a Frenchman who was leader of the Protestant Reformation in France and Switzerland. Calvinists wore very simple clothes and wanted worship to be a serious no-frills business. Spoilsports.

Catholicism A branch of Christianity. Its leader, the Pope, was (and still is) seen as God's Representative on Earth. Its full title is 'Roman Catholicism' and it's seen as 'High Church' with plenty of statues, incense and praying to saints.

Heir presumptive A person who expects to succeed a monarch (in the case of Mary, hoping to succeed Queen Elizabeth I of England) but may be ruled out by the birth of someone with a stronger claim to the throne (e.g. if Elizabeth had married and had a child).

Protestantism The branch of Christianity which is made up of all the Christians who aren't Roman Catholics. These include: Episcopalians, Quakers, Presbyterians, Puritans and Calvinists, and that's just a few. A real mixed bag.

Quadrangle A rectangular courtyard, usually with buildings on all four sides. Thrilling, huh?

Ratify To give formal approval to. Once treaties and agreements were signed, it was often still up to the monarch to ratify them – giving them the final 'OK'.

Regent Someone who rules on behalf of the monarch, usually if the monarch is too ill, too mad or too young (or sometimes all three).

Rosary A string of beads used by Catholics to count a special series of prayers which are also called 'the rosary'.

Rosery A garden full of roses. (Just thought I'd mention it.)

Scottish Reformation The 're-forming' of Scotland from a Catholic to a Protestant state.

MARY – THE TODDLER YEARS

Mary Queen of Scots wasn't born 'Mary Queen of Scots' but 'Mary Stuart'. She was the daughter of King James V of Scotland and his French wife, Mary of Guise. Mary – *our* Mary – was born on either the 7th or 8th of December 1542, at the palace of Linlithgow. No one seems to be sure which date it was but, with 8 December being the Feast of the Immaculate Conception of the Virgin Mary, Mary herself always called the 8th her birthday.

RUMOUR, RUMOUR EVERYWHERE

Mary had hardly been born before rumours started spreading about her. One was that she was terribly frail, another was that she was dead, and yet another rumour was that she was, in fact, a boy. It depended upon who you were as to which rumour you chose to believe! The Scots wanted to believe their royal baby was a boy, so that their king would have a son and heir. The English (under King Henry VIII) wanted to believe the child dead, so that James V of Scotland would have no one to succeed him. Another rumour was that the baby had been christened Elizabeth, the name of her cousin whom – if you stick around to find out – was to be the person behind her tragic downfall. (Sob! Wail!)

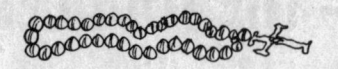

THE ENGLISH AND THE SCOTS

Today, England and Scotland are a part of what we call the United Kingdom, but back then they weren't. Although King Henry VIII of England was the uncle of Mary's dad, there was no love lost between them or between the English and the Scots. They were sworn enemies. Henry VIII of England had three children by three different wives: Mary Tudor (yup, another Mary, just to make things confusing), Elizabeth and Edward.

THE WORST OF TIMES

Mary – yes, *our* Mary, later Queen of Scots – was born just a few days after a battle between the Scottish and the English. The Battle of Solway Moss, as it became known, was a terrible defeat for her father's troops. Many Scotsmen died and, equally embarrassingly, over 1,000 Scottish noblemen were taken back to London as prisoners. King James V was horrified and heartbroken. He went to bed and never got up again, dying of shame on 14 December 1542. Both of Mary's brothers had died as babies before she was born so, less than a week after her birth, Mary Stuart was now Queen Mary of Scotland or, to put it another way, Mary Queen of Scots.

> WE CHARGE AT THE ENGLISH ON MY COUNT. ONE, TWO ...

TO RULE IN HER STEAD

With Mary Queen of Scots just a tiny baby, the most pressing matter was who should rule Scotland on her behalf? Her mother couldn't, of course. Things just weren't done that way. There were two separate claims as to how this job should be carried out. The Earl of Arran claimed that he should be sole regent until Mary was old enough to rule Scotland herself because, as head of the house of Hamilton, this was his hereditary right. The Hamilton Clan were another branch of the Scottish royal family. A cardinal called Beaton, however, claimed that Scotland shouldn't be ruled by one man but be overseen by a council of five governors (one of which would, indeed, be Arran), with the cardinal at its head! Cardinal Beaton claimed that this was what King James V had wanted and produced a will to prove it.

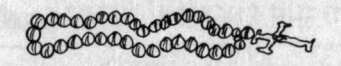

UNRELIABLE EARL & CRAFTY CARDINAL

The Earl of Arran was an important man and, if Mary Queen of Scots died, he had a perfectly good claim to the throne of Scotland in his own right. As choice for sole regent, though, he was far from ideal. He was notoriously indecisive and unreliable, if not a little unstable. Cardinal Beaton, the Archbishop of St Andrews, was unreliable in another way. This so-called will of the late King James V he'd produced was very probably a forgery.

VICTORY AND ARREST

Unreliable or not, the Earl of Arran won the day and became sole regent of Scotland, to rule on Mary's behalf until she 'came of age'. Cardinal Beaton, meanwhile, was arrested. The Scottish noblemen who'd been taken prisoner after the Battle of Solway Moss had been released by Henry VIII of England and returned to Scotland.

Whilst in England, many of these men had become sympathetic to Henry's Protestant, English cause, and didn't want to see a Catholic cardinal with so much influence in Scotland. The Earl of Arran himself had abandoned his Catholic faith.

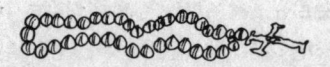

CHURCH OF ENGLAND, CHURCH OF ROME

Like most of Europe, England had been a Catholic country, answerable to the Catholic Church and His Holiness the Pope in Rome. Following, amongst other things, his difficulty in divorcing his first wife, Henry VIII of England had broken free of the Pope and the Roman Catholic Church, putting himself at the head of his own church in his own country. The Scottish monarchy, meanwhile – if not all the Scots themselves – remained staunchly Catholic and Mary's mother and late father were no exception. With James V dead and Mary still a baby, much Scottish power now lay with pro-Protestant noblemen.

A MARRIAGE OF CONVENIENCE

King Henry VIII of England was now ready to push matters even further. He wanted to be absolutely sure of his power over the troublesome Scots just north of the border. The young – and, boy do I mean *young* – Mary Queen of Scots presented him with an ideal opportunity. What if Henry VIII's son Edward, heir to the English throne, was to marry Mary when they were both old enough? That way, their two countries could become united and, being the male, Edward would, in effect, become king of both countries too. Although Mary wasn't yet a year old, and Edward not yet six, the Treaties of Greenwich were drawn up on 1 July 1543, betrothing them to each other. Mary's mother and the Scottish court couldn't really say 'no'. They'd recently been defeated by Henry, remember.

THE TIDE TURNS

By the summer of 1543, Cardinal Beaton – whose first name was David, by the way, should anyone ask – was a free man, having somehow managed to escape from his imprisonment. He spent much of his time preaching pro-Catholic, pro-French ideas. Why pro-French? Because the French were Catholics, because Mary's mother was French and because the French were the worst enemies of Henry

VIII and the English. Two other influential pro-Catholic, pro-French Scotsmen were the Earl of Arran's own half-brother, the Abbot of Paisley, and the Earl of Lennox. All of them managed to influence the sole governor, Arran, that perhaps sucking up to the Protestant English wasn't such a good idea after all.

A PLACE OF SAFETY

The ink was barely dry on the Treaties of Greenwich when news reached Henry VIII in England that there were French ships just off the Scottish coast. Henry was worried that they were coming to try to snatch the baby Mary Queen of Scots. He sent word to Scotland that she must be moved from Linlithgow Palace to somewhere safer. The decision was, indeed, then made to move her . . . but to protect Mary from the English as much as the French! On 21 July 1543, Cardinal Beaton and 7,000 loyal Catholic followers marched from Stirling to Linlithgow, to insist that Mary come back with them and live in Stirling Castle.

A MIGHTY STRONGHOLD

High above Stirling town, Stirling Castle was thought to be one of the safest castles in Scotland, with a commanding view of any approaching enemies, and with impressive defences. Once safely inside, Henry VIII wanted baby Mary to be in the care of his own envoy, the Englishman Sir Ralph Sadler. After all, she would be married to his son one day, so didn't Henry have a right to demand such things? The Scots didn't think so. Mary's four guardians were to be the Scottish lords: Graham, Lindsay, Livingston (without an 'e') and Erskine, all chosen by the pro-Arran Protestant Earl of Glencairn.

CORONATION STATIONS

History might have turned out very different if Henry VIII of England hadn't finally gone too far. At one stage he tried to bribe Cardinal Beaton to give up his life in the Catholic Church and to throw in his lot with the English. Then the English impounded a Scottish merchant ship due to trade with the English's dreaded enemies, the French . . . and the Earl of Arran finally decided that enough was enough. On 8 September 1543, the regent attended a Catholic mass and switched his support to Cardinal Beaton and the pro-French. The following day, the nine-month-old Mary was crowned queen.

THE FRENCH CONNECTION

Now that the Scots were allies of the French and now that the dauphin, Prince Henri, and Catherine de' Medici of France had had a little baby boy – Francis, in January 1544

– the idea that Mary should marry the English heir Edward seemed crazy. Surely it made much more sense for the Catholic, half-French Mary Queen of Scots to be engaged to the dauphin's Catholic, French son? It was simple speculation at this stage, but it soon reached Henry VIII's ears and he didn't like what he heard.

ENGLAND'S REVENGE

Henry VIII could see that all his Scottish scheming was getting him exactly nowhere. His plans were falling apart around him, so he needed to act. He decided his best approach was to make the Scottish realize just how ruthless and powerful the English were. He would try to woo them (win them over) with a show of strength, not promises. The terror which followed, therefore, became known as the 'rough wooing'. Homes, villages, farmland and gardens were laid waste. Even the city of Edinburgh was burnt and the abbey and Holyrood Palace ransacked. The English later captured merchant ships and even vandalized the tombs of ancient Scottish heroes.

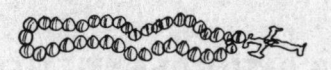

ENEMIES WITHIN

The English weren't the only cause of unrest in Scotland, however. There were those Scots who were unhappy with the power and wealth of the Catholic Church in their country. In March 1546, for example, a Protestant preacher named George Wishart was burnt at St Andrews Castle watched by, amongst others, Cardinal Beaton and his bishops. Three months later, it was the cardinal's turn to come to a sticky end. Disguised as masons sent to repair the castle, a group of Scottish Lords from Fife stabbed the cardinal, took over the castle and hung his naked and horribly mutilated body from one of its towers for all to see. Later, the body was taken down and pickled in a barrel of salt - yes, that's what I said: *pickled in a barrel of salt* - and kept in the 'Bottle Dungeon' for a year or so! The Earl of Arran's forces laid siege to the castle which held out against them for an impressive fourteen months. It came to an end on 30 July 1547 when French forces intervened. Many of those defenders who weren't executed were taken as prisoners to France.

THE BATTLE OF PINKIE CLEUGH

1547 was also the year that saw England's most serious assault on Mary's Scotland so far. The Scots knew that an attack was coming and about 36,000 people, from all four corners of the country – if Scotland has corners – headed for Edinburgh. The battle actually took place at Pinkie Cleugh, near the town of Musselburgh. The Scottish forces were up on a ridge, under the command of the Earl of Arran himself. It was a strong, defensive position, so your guess is as good as mine why the earl chose to *attack* instead! The English troops were far better trained and slaughtered the Scots.

MAKE INCHMAHONE MY HOME!

With the English commander, Somerset, on the loose in the Scottish lowlands, it was decided that Stirling Castle was no longer the safest place for Mary Queen of Scots to be. Still under five years old, the queen was moved to a priory on Inchmahone, which was a tiny island in a lake not far from Stirling. She was only there for about three weeks but, because it was such a fairytale setting, many myths have grown up about her time there. In fact, she was soon back at Stirling and, in February 1548, was moved to Dumbarton Castle on the west coast.

I KNOW THEY SAID IT WAS A CASTLE ON A TINY ISLAND...BUT I IMAGINED SOMETHING A BIT BIGGER!

TO THE RESCUE!

By July 1548, Prince Henri, the dauphin, had become King Henri II of France and Catherine de' Medici his queen. Their son Francis was now dauphin and it was agreed that Mary Queen of Scots should become engaged to *him* instead of the English prince. The French also agreed to defend Scotland against the English if needs be.

SAD FAREWELLS

If Mary was to marry the new dauphin, then it was agreed that she must be brought up in the French court. In July, one of King Henri II of France's own ships arrived, with escorts, at Dumbarton on the west coast. Sadly, Mary's own mother, Mary of Guise, was to remain in Scotland. It would be the responsibility of the French king and queen to bring up little Mary. Life could be very tough like that, when it came to arranged marriages. So, on 29 July 1548, Mary said a sad farewell to her mum, and climbed aboard the ship, ready to set sail for France and a new chapter in her life . . .

EN FRANCE
(AS THE FRENCH SAY)

Although Mary's mum was French, Mary could only speak Scots when she arrived in France, which is fair enough if you're five and Scottish. After a stormy crossing – during which it was reported that she was the only one who wasn't seasick – Mary took to France like a duck to water. This is hardly surprising, because King Henri and Queen Catherine made her so welcome. Later, the king described her as being 'the most perfect child I have ever seen'.

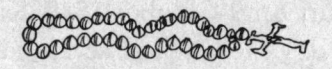

THE FOUR MARIES

Amongst plenty of other things, Mary Queen of Scots is famous for being accompanied to France by the 'Four Maries'. All of noble birth, they were: Mary Beaton, Mary Fleming, Mary Livingston (without an 'e') and Mary Seton . . . as if there weren't enough people called Mary in this book already! Before you ask: yes, Mary Beaton was a relative of Cardinal Beaton, but she was from a different branch of the family; and, yes, Mary Livingston (without an 'e') was related to the Lord Livingston (without an 'e') named in the bogus will of James V as one of the proposed five governors of Scotland, who had since - by the way - become one of Mary's guardians. Mary Fleming was of 'royal Scottish blood' and Mary Seton's mother, a Frenchwoman, had first come to Scotland as a lady-in-waiting to Mary's own mother. It was a small world!

> RIGHT, THIS WAY, WE GET TO REMEMBER WHO'S WHO ON THIS VOYAGE!

Kween — wun — tew — three — faw

IN COURT AT LAST

After two months in France, Mary finally arrived at the French royal court on 9 October 1548. King Henri and his wife Catherine de' Medici had seven children altogether. After Francis (the dauphin) came Elisabeth – no, not that one, you're thinking of Henry VIII of England's daughter – Claude (a girl), Charles, Henry, another Francis and, last but not least, Marguerite. None of them was in the best of health.

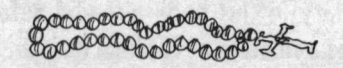

NOT TRUE! NOT TRUE!

No book about Mary Queen of Scots would be complete without the marmalade myth, even though it's not true. The story goes that the ever-popular young Mary was ill in bed and, down in the palace kitchens a sad chef was stirring a bowl of oranges, muttering 'Marie est malade', which is French for 'Mary is ill', over and over again as he stirred. Suddenly he noticed that the oranges had became what we now think of as marmalade. He had invented a new treat, which he named especially after the occasion! The truth be told, the word 'marmalade' comes from the Portuguese word for a fruit called a quince – not from 'Marie est malade' – and marmalade had been around for years by then anyway!

FRIENDSHIPS ARE FORMED

With the Four Maries sent to be educated at the convent of Poissy by nuns, Mary had to make new friends. Her best friend was Princess Elisabeth. She didn't actually meet Elisabeth's father, the king, until November and he was instantly charmed by her. As she quickly learnt French, the two would sometimes talk for hours. The next ten years or so were the most carefree in her life.

A VISIT FROM HER MOTHER

In September 1550, Mary's mother, Mary of Guise, came to the French court to see her. Mary was overjoyed! This would be the first time they'd met in over two years. Mother and daughter were delighted to be reunited and Mary of Guise was made very welcome by King Henri and Queen Catherine. Mary's mum stayed for a year before heading back to Scotland, via London.

MARRIAGE AT LAST

Unlike the proposed marriage between Mary Queen of Scots and Prince Edward of England, the marriage between Mary Queen of Scots and the dauphin, Francis, did take place. On Sunday 24 April 1558 Mary (aged fifteen) and Francis (aged fourteen) were married in the famous cathedral of Notre Dame, following their official engagement on 19 April. This had resulted from plenty of behind-the-scenes wheeler-dealing between French officials and Scottish envoys, led by Mary's granny, Antoinette of Guise. Antoinette was acting on behalf of Mary's mum, who'd become Scotland's regent, governing the country until Mary was old enough.

THE TWO TREATIES

Before Mary and Francis were married, Scottish envoys signed a treaty with the French agreeing what would happen if one or the other died. It was all fair and square. But what they didn't know about was the *second* treaty. These secret papers contained far more explosive agreements between Mary Queen of Scots and the French

... and, when you read what she agreed to, you'll see why it was so hush hush. First off, it was agreed that if Mary died without children, Scotland would automatically be governed by France (becoming little more than a French province). Secondly, Scotland, its treasury and income would be handed over to France until every penny that France had spent on defending it had been repaid (which the French could make sure was never). And, finally, whatever agreements Mary might enter into later that went against what was agreed here would be null and void ... which was very far-sighted and sneaky of them. It may seem amazing that Mary agreed to sign these arrangements, but it's worth remembering that she was still just a girl and loved and trusted those around her.

DEATH OF 'THE OTHER' MARY

In November 1558, events in England became very important to Mary Queen of Scots. The English monarch, Queen Mary [Tudor], Henry VIII's Roman Catholic daughter, died. King Henri II of France now declared his daughter-in-law, *our* Mary, to be Queen of England as well as Scotland. He insisted she use the English royal coat-of-arms as her own. The English, meanwhile, crowned Mary Tudor's half-sister 'Queen Elizabeth of England'.

THE STUART CLAIM

So what made the French king think Mary Queen of Scots had a right to the English throne? Let me try to explain. Here goes: Mary Tudor's dad and mum were Henry VIII and Catherine of Aragon. Henry then divorced Catherine and married Anne Boleyn. They had a daughter, Elizabeth. In the eyes of the Catholic Church, however, there was no such thing as divorce, so Henry was still married to Aragon which meant that Elizabeth was illegitimate – born outside marriage – so couldn't inherit the English throne. Who did that leave? Well, Mary Queen of Scots's great-grandfather was Elizabeth's grandfather, King Henry VII of England so, the French argued, Mary was the only legitimate, living descendant of that king and should, therefore, be crowned Queen of England. Simple ... I *don't* think.

ANOTHER DEATH, ANOTHER CROWN

Soon another death led to far more immediate changes for our Mary. In June 1559, King Henri II of France was enjoying a good day's jousting. To round off the day, he challenged Jacques de Lorge, the Count of Montgomery, to one last joust. According to some versions of events, Queen Catherine de' Medici pleaded with her husband not to, having had two premonitions that this would end in disaster. Montgomery is supposed to have refused to fight, until his king ordered him to . . . As it was, Montgomery's lance shattered, one huge splinter piercing the king's eye and the other his throat. He died on 10 July. Mary's husband was no longer dauphin but King of France. She was now its sixteen-year-old queen.

MARY – QUEEN OF FRANCE

Sadly, this is one of the shortest chapters in any *GET A LIFE!* biography so far. The reason is simple. Mary Queen of Scots wasn't to be Mary Queen of France for very long.

A BAD YEAR

The year 1560 was a terrible one for Mary. In June, her mum, Mary of Guise, died back in Scotland. When Mary heard the news she was heartbroken. Meanwhile, matters with England were still high on the agenda and, in July, it was agreed in the Treaty of Edinburgh that English troops would leave Scotland, so long as French troops did the same – with a few agreed exceptions – and that Mary and Francis would give up any claim to the English throne and recognize Elizabeth as England's rightful queen. At the same time, both England and France would promise to stay out of Scottish affairs. The English troops did withdraw, but matters were then messed up when the Scottish Reformation burst onto the scene. Suddenly, Scotland was a Protestant country with a Catholic queen away in France. With Elizabeth being a Protestant queen, the Scots would be more likely to turn to *her* for help when needed than their own 'true' queen on the Continent.

NOT THE HEALTHIEST OF CHAPS

Then there were the worries about Francis. The king had never been the healthiest of people (neither had Mary). He fainted on more than one occasion and his face was covered with worrying looking blotches. Wild rumours spread around France that he had leprosy. Even worse, stories were told that he often washed in children's blood to try to cure himself! This was totally untrue, of course, but enough to make some people hide their kids when the young king was around! Crowned King Francis II on 18 September 1559, Mary's young husband died on 5 December 1560. Mary was Queen of France no longer. End of chapter.

PLANS FOR THE FUTURE

Nowadays it is customary for those in mourning for the dead to wear black. Although Mary shut herself away in a black room, talking to as few people as possible, she chose to wear *white* for the forty days of official mourning. There was little reason for her to remain in France after that, though. Francis's brother, Charles, was now King Charles IX, with her mother-in-law Catherine de' Medici acting as unofficial regent, governing the country on his behalf. What role was there for Mary?

MARRIAGE WITH SPAIN?

Mary's attentions were now turned to Spain, however. She was considering the possibility of marrying Don Carlos, heir to the Spanish throne with its mighty empire. Spain was a great power, and like Mary, Don Carlos was a Catholic. Not only that, the weather in Spain was much warmer and more pleasant than in Scotland, which she might otherwise return to. The downside was that, although the Spanish heir was sixteen, he weighed only five and a half stone and – after falling down stairs when chasing after a chambermaid – he often had fits of homicidal mania. (In other words, he'd try to kill people.) If that wasn't sad and bad enough, he'd fallen head-over-heels in love with his own stepmother! Not the ideal choice for Husband Number Two, perhaps?

ENGLAND SUCKS UP

The English court was eager to have Mary on their side and the Earl of Bedford was sent to France in February 1561, to offer Queen Elizabeth's condolences at the death of her husband. A young Englishman named Lord Darnley also paid a visit, at his mother's request.

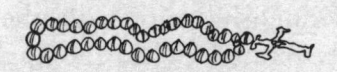

DASHING DARNLEY

Lord Darnley was, in fact, a title. His family name was Henry Stuart and he and Mary Queen of Scots shared the same grandmother, Margaret Tudor, which made them cousins. (Whereas Mary's grandfather had been Margaret's first husband, King James IV of Scotland, *his* grandfather had been her second husband, the 6th Earl of Angus.) He had royal Scottish AND English blood in him. Darnley had first met Mary at her husband Francis's coronation. His mother had sent Darnley back to France in the hope that her dashing son might be considered a good prospect as a second husband for Mary. But Mary wasn't interested in Lord Darnley yet. [Y-E-T.]

HER MIND IS MADE UP

Mary could have stayed in France as a dowager queen – widow of a dead monarch – for the rest of her days. But, for whatever reason, she decided to return 'home' to the country she hadn't set foot in since she was a tiny tot. But first Mary wanted Queen Elizabeth of England to guarantee her 'safe passage'. Mary sent an envoy named d'Oysel to the English court with the request, which Elizabeth blankly refused. When the English ambassador, Sir Nicholas Throckmorton, heard the news, he was puzzled. Surely it would be better for England for Mary to be nearer to home and out of the way up in Scotland, rather than in the thick of things on the Continent?

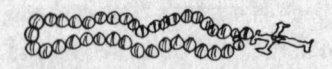

THE UNRESOLVED TREATY

Another sticking point between Elizabeth Queen of England and Mary Queen of Scots went all the way back to the Treaty of Edinburgh in July 1560 (and all the way back to page 138). As you may remember, all was going fine until the Scottish Reformation meant that not everything agreed in the treaty was put into action. As a result, Mary had never bothered to ratify the treaty for the Scots. Ratify means 'give the final OK to', so, without Mary's ratification, the treaty was never officially and finally agreed. It had been one of Throckmorton's many jobs to persuade Mary to ratify it now.

ALL ABOARD!

Mary now took a more informal approach, writing Queen Elizabeth a personal letter, in the friendliest of terms, asking for safe passage... but didn't wait for a reply before acting. She said her 'goodbyes' then prepared to leave. As well as three of her uncles, Mary travelled back to Scotland with the 'Four Maries' she'd first come over with: Seton, Beaton, Livingston and Fleming.

It had been suggested to our Mary that she leave her jewellery behind for safety's sake. She was quick to point out that, if the ship was safe enough for her, it was safe enough for her jewels! Now, she was heading home...

BACK HOME

Mary's ships did indeed run into English ships on the voyage home, but only to send her greetings. Queen Elizabeth of England had responded to Mary's latest letter in a friendly manner. On Tuesday 19 August 1561, Mary set foot on Scottish soil for the first time in thirteen years, after landing at the port of Leith. It was nine o'clock in the morning, the place was thick with mist and no one had expected her to arrive so soon. There were no large crowds to greet her and no lodging had been arranged for her. She had lunch and a quick nap at the home of one Andrew Lamb.

TO HOLYROOD!

After this, Mary Queen of Scots was escorted to Holyrood Palace, just outside the walls of the city of Edinburgh. She was flanked by a number of Scottish lords, including the Protestant Earl of Argyll and a man named James Stewart who was, in fact, her half-brother.

Even though Scotland was now pretty much ruled by the Protestant Church, guided by the Protestant reformer John Knox – ignore the 'K', it was pronounced 'nox' – and though Mary herself was Catholic, there was a fair bit of rejoicing at their queen's arrival. Bonfires were lit to celebrate her return.

A RESTLESS NIGHT

Mary's first night back in Scotland, in her suite of rooms at Holyrood, is famous for its awfulness. Five or six hundred well-wishers gathered outside the palace and began playing and singing psalms to welcome Mary Queen of Scots home. The singing was, apparently, tuneless and the playing dreadful too. Legend has it that it was the sound of the bagpipes that kept Mary awake but, in fact, the crowd played fiddles and another type of stringed instrument called a rebec. The next morning, Queen Mary diplomatically pronounced that the experience had been a delight!

CATHOLIC CAPERS

Mary thought that she was being equally diplomatic when it came to practising her religion. She would stick to her Catholic beliefs but perform the rights – attend mass and so on – in private. Despite this, when news leaked out that their queen was to attend her first mass in the 'chapel royal' in the palace, angry Protestant reformers tried to burst in, but were prevented by her half-brother! Mary was quick to act. She made it clear that no one (including her) would interfere with the new state religion of Protestantism, on the pain of death, but, at the same time, no one must interfere with the beliefs of those Catholics who'd come back from France . . . also on the pain of death. John Knox was far from thrilled.

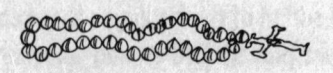

JOHN KNOX

John Knox had started life as a Catholic but ended up supporting the murderers of Cardinal Beaton in St Andrew's Castle and was taken prisoner. Later, he went to Protestant England but, when Catholic Mary Tudor became queen, he'd nipped over to the Continent, where he became a Calvinist. Returning to Scotland, he converted many people to Protestantism, preached violence and openly hated Mary.

BUILDING BRIDGES

Neither 'side' did the other any favours, and Mary spent many of her first months in Scotland trying to find a fair balance for both Protestants and Catholics. At the same time, she was eager to build a friendship with her cousin, Queen Elizabeth, over in England. Less than two weeks after her return home, Mary sent William Maitland to the English court as her envoy. The main aim was simple: if Mary ratified the treaty of Edinburgh for Elizabeth (that business on page 142), Elizabeth should officially recognize Mary as next in line to the English throne if she, Elizabeth, had no children to succeed her. Although Queen Elizabeth was quick to stress that she'd far rather Mary succeed her than some of the other possibilities, she wouldn't commit herself to declaring a choice publicly. She claimed that if she agreed to this, Mary would probably end up the centre of attention for plots to overthrow her and to put Mary on the throne of England.

MR & MRS QUEEN

Although both wanted something from the other – Elizabeth wanted Mary to ratify a slightly revised Treaty of Edinburgh and Mary wanted to be recognized as 'heir presumptive' – they wrote a series of friendly letters to each other, for a while. Mary is said to have said as a joke that it was a pity that neither she nor Elizabeth was a man because, if one them had been, then they could have got married and unified the thrones of England and Scotland. This had already occurred to Nicholas Throckmorton!

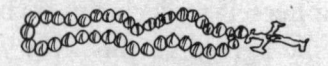

SCOTS PLOTS

At this time, all was not peace and quiet in Scotland either. There were many plots between groups of Protestant Scottish nobles trying to discredit Catholic Scottish nobles, and vice versa. The 3rd Earl of Arran sent a coded message stating that the Earl of Bothwell had tried to get him involved in a plot to kidnap Mary and rule Scotland in her place! Arran's own family thought him quite mad, and had already locked him up in the family castle. Despite this, Mary had Bothwell locked up in Edinburgh Castle, just in case. Arran managed to escape from his prison in real comic-book style. He really did climb out of the window on a rope made out of sheets knotted together!

GHASTLY GORDON

In August 1562, Mary paid her first visit to the highlands of her kingdom. Here, she ran into a spot of bother with Sir John Gordon, one of the twelve children of the 4th Earl of Huntly. Gordon planned to abduct the queen for real, and followed the royal party. Rumour spread that 1,000 horsemen from the Gordon clan were waiting to pounce but, if they were, they never put in an appearance. Huntly and Gordon were soon declared outlaws. The Earl promptly died of a heart attack when faced by troops loyal to Queen Mary. His dead body was then embalmed and brought to the Scottish Parliament to be tried for treason. His corpse was found guilty and beheaded!!! It was a living Sir John Gordon who was executed in the queen's presence. The executioner did such a botched job that Mary broke down and wept.

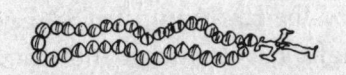

ANOTHER NUTTER?

Amongst the party who'd come from France to Scotland with Mary Queen of Scots was the Frenchman Pierre de Châtelard. He soon declared an undying passion for the queen, and she seemed to like his harmless flirting ... until he was caught hiding under her bed and she had him kicked out of court. The following night he burst in on her, and Mary called for her half-brother (now the Earl of Moray) to stab him. Instead, Châtelard was publicly tried and executed. Had he been a madman, genuinely believing he was in love with the queen? Or had he been out to ruin her reputation? No one knows.

HUNT FOR A HUBBY

Mary hadn't given up hope in the hunt for a husband and let everyone know that she still hadn't ruled out the possibility of marrying Don Carlos of Spain. John Knox was horrified at the thought of her marrying another *Catholic*. Queen Elizabeth of England was horrified too, and was swift to act. Knowing that her cousin Mary was keen to be named 'heir presumptive' of England, Elizabeth thought she might have enough influence over her to be able to get involved in a little matchmaking. Having sworn that she'd never marry anyone herself, Elizabeth suggested her own favourite, Lord Robert Dudley, as a husband to Mary.

DASHING DARNLEY RETURNS

Then, in February 1565, Mary's cousin, dashing Lord Darnley, suddenly paid a visit to Scotland. Whether it was Elizabeth or some of her advisers who were trying to push forward Darnley is uncertain . . . but it had the desired effect. Mary really took a liking to him after he fell ill at Stirling Castle. She spent more and more time at his bedside and fell head-over-heels in love with him. All thoughts of carefully arranged, politically clever marriages were forgotten. She would marry Darnley whatever the cost.

DARNLEY TURNS DASTARDLY

And marry they did, in July 1565, despite the fact that it nearly led to civil war in Scotland. Darnley was another Catholic, and she even gave him the title 'King of Scotland'. The Protestants were outraged. Suddenly, Mary's own half-brother would have nothing to do with her. Darnley, meanwhile, revealed his nastier side. He was a cruel, drunken swine. Upset and pregnant, Mary turned to her secretary, David Rizzio – sometimes spelled Riccio – for comfort. Egged on by certain Scottish lords (and convinced that Mary was being more than just comforted by Rizzio), Darnley arranged for the secretary's murder.

I NEVER SAW THIS NASTY SIDE OF YOU BEFORE WE MARRIED, DARNLEY!

EXIT RIZZIO

On 9 March 1566, Mary was having supper with Rizzio and a group of friends in her suite in Holyrood Palace.

Suddenly, Darnley burst in from his private staircase, followed closely by Lord Ruthven. Darnley stood in front of his pregnant wife, preventing her from helping her poor secretary, whilst Ruthven stabbed Rizzio over fifty – yes FIFTY – times. (Some say as many as sixty.) Though shocked and horrified, with the dying Rizzio clutching the hem of her dress, Mary was herself unhurt. She gave birth to a healthy baby, James, three months later. Darnley claimed he'd been shielding his wife from Ruthven to protect her. Mary wasn't so sure.

AMBITIOUS BOTHWELL

Not surprisingly, Mary now hated Darnley, but what could she do? She turned to the Earl of Bothwell for help. After weeping at Rizzio's murder, Mary said, 'No more tears now; I will think upon revenge'. And revenge was what she would have. The Earl of Bothwell was the same Bothwell who'd been thrown into Edinburgh Castle without trial back on page 148. By now he was back in the queen's favour.

UNDER THE WEATHER

With her son and heir, James, safely tucked away at Stirling Castle, under the care of the Earl of Mar and the Erskine family, Mary made it clear that it was James who would succeed her, not her husband Darnley. Mary was ill and, in an age when people were far more likely to die from an illness, she was obviously concerned to make this matter v-e-r-y c-l-e-a-r. Throughout her illness, Darnley didn't bother to pretend to be a devoted husband, so didn't even visit her once.

THE DEATH OF DIABOLICAL DARNLEY

The following January, 1567, Darnley fell ill in Glasgow and Mary was kind enough to send her doctor to him – they were no longer living together. She later set out to bring him back to Edinburgh to get better. He chose to stay in a house just on the edge of the city in a quadrangle known as the Kirk o' Fields.

At about two o'clock one February morning, there was a huge explosion at the house. Darnley's body either went flying out of the bed, up in the air and landed some distance away with what would have been a very nasty squelch . . . or it was placed there to look like that had happened (and the explosion had been designed to cover up the real murder) . . . or he'd heard the explosives being planted, had tried to escape and had been caught. Either way, it wasn't the explosion that killed him – he had been suffocated first.

MARY IN MOURNING . . . AGAIN

Mary Queen of Scots went into mourning once more, this time wearing the more traditional black. Many people have argued that she was either behind the plot to kill Darnley, or knew about it, because it was public knowledge that the explosion was arranged by Bothwell and a group of Scottish lords. But just how involved was the queen? Nowadays, many historians argue that Mary probably didn't know what Bothwell was up to. In March, a private prosecution of Bothwell was brought before parliament, but he was found 'not guilty' and acquitted.

BAD TO WORSE

On 21 April 1567, Mary visited her baby, James, at Stirling Castle. She played with him the whole of the next day too, blissfully unaware that this would be the very last time that they would be together. She would never see her son again. On the 23rd, Mary headed for home. Unwell, she was travelling with a party of just over 300 people, which was considered a small number for a royal party. On 24 April, about six miles from Edinburgh, Bothwell appeared with a private army of 800 men . . .

A KIDNAP BY ANY OTHER NAME

Although Bothwell claimed that there was 'danger' in Edinburgh and that he'd come to take Mary to Dunbar Castle where she'd be out of harm's way, it was clear what he was up to. He planned to kidnap his queen, and many of Mary's party realized this and were prepared to fight. Heavily outnumbered, eager to avoid bloodshed and resigned to her fate, Mary agreed to go with Bothwell. Back in Edinburgh, the alarm was raised and a rescue was planned. But it was too late to thwart Bothwell's scheme.

By amazing coincidence Mary's kidnap took place on the ninth anniversary of her marriage to her first husband, Francis.

HUSBAND NUMBER THREE

Astonishingly, on 15 May 1567, Bothwell now married Mary at Holyrood! Did he force her or had she fallen in love with him? Who knows . . . the outcome was still the same. The Scots were horrified. Mary's previous husband had only been dead for three months and, more likely than not, he'd been murdered by the man she was now married to! And Bothwell had had to divorce his own sick wife to marry Mary. The Protestant lords now united against them.

DEFEAT!

On Sunday 15 June, the rebel army marched out of Edinburgh. They met Bothwell's 'royal' troops at Carberry Hill. Mary was eventually captured and taken back to Edinburgh. Along the way, she was showered with insults. The most common cry seems to have been 'Murderess!'. After Edinburgh, she became a prisoner in a castle on an island in the middle of Lochleven and forced to abdicate – to give up the throne. Bothwell, meanwhile, fled the country. On 29 July 1567, Mary's son – just over a year old – was crowned King James VI of Scotland. To some, our Mary was no longer seen as 'Queen of Scots'.

WILY WILLY!

Even though Mary was stuck on an island in a middle of a loch miles from Edinburgh, she wasn't without friends. After ten months' imprisonment, a group of them helped her to escape. In the castle there were members of the Douglas family, including one young Willy Douglas. A May Day pageant at the castle was arranged for 2 May 1568 and there were plenty of strangers about. Willy stole a set of keys to the main gates and had Mary boldly walk right through them, in disguise. She was then bundled into a boat and rowed to freedom. Willy Douglas remained in Mary's service right up until she died.

A FINAL STAND

Mary still had her supporters *outside* the castle too. She'd soon gathered together an army of 5,000 loyal Scots and went to face her half-brother (the Earl of Moray)'s army of about 3,000 at the village of Langside. Mary's troops were under the command of the Earl of Argyll and, unfortunately, he either fainted or deliberately betrayed the queen. (After all, the Earl of Moray was his brother-in-law!) The result was a defeat for Mary. She fled.

DECISIONS, DECISIONS

Now Mary had to make one of the momentous decisions of her life. She didn't feel she could stay in Scotland any longer, but where should she go? The obvious answer was France. It was a Catholic country where she'd once been queen and they were bound to support her against the Protestants. Instead, Mary decided to seek sanctuary in England. It was a Protestant country ruled by a queen she'd never met and with whom she'd often disagreed. But Mary's mind was made up. Perhaps she held out the hope that she might one day rule England after all.

A FINAL FAREWELL

On Sunday 16 May 1568, Mary stepped into a fishing boat and, at three o'clock, left the shores of Scotland for the very last time. The journey across the Solway Firth was only four hours and England loomed ever-larger up ahead of her. With her were about twenty loyal followers and servants. There was no turning back.

MARY IN MERRIE ENGLAND

Once in England – Mary landed in Cumberland (not to be muddled with *Cu*cumberland, home of the long green vegetable) – she immediately wrote to her cousin, Queen Elizabeth, for help. Finding herself held a semi-prisoner in Carlisle Castle, Mary awaited news from the English court. Not surprisingly, the Protestant Queen Elizabeth had no intention of helping the Catholic Mary reclaim the throne of Scotland by force. And, anyway, wasn't it quite useful having her locked up where she couldn't do any mischief?

DARN IT, DARNLEY!

Then there was the small matter of whether Mary had played a part in the murder of Lord Darnley and the fact that she'd ended up marrying Bothwell, the number one suspect!!! Queen Elizabeth declared that Mary must allow her to judge her innocence or guilt before deciding to welcome her with open arms. Mary was furious.

THE CASE FOR THE DEFENCE

Mary was moved to Bolton Castle in Yorkshire. This, Elizabeth claimed, was so that Mary would be that bit nearer the English court . . . but it was still a good way off! Then the Conference of York began in October 1568. During the conference, an English panel, under the Duke of Norfolk, examined the evidence for and against Mary in the case of Darnley's murder. The case against Mary was brought by her own half-brother, the Earl of Moray, who was now regent to her son, King James VI. She was represented by a number of commissioners.

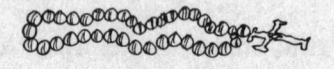

> AND THIS WILL BE YOUR ROOM, YOUR MAJESTY.
>
> I'M NOTHING BUT A PRISONER!
>
> WHATEVER GAVE YOU THAT IDEA?

THE CASKET LETTERS

The Protestant Scots had produced a casket which, according to them, was jam-packed full of letters from Mary to Bothwell, supposedly 'proving' that she and Bothwell had been in love from the start and had plotted to kill Darnley together. These were presented to the panel at the conference and threw everyone into such turmoil that Queen Elizabeth ordered a new conference to be set up in Westminster. Today, the general opinion amongst most historians is that the 'casket letters' were in fact forgeries/ fakes/made-up/whopping great lies.

THE VERDICT

The panel's verdict when it came was very wishy-washy to say the least. In the end, Queen Elizabeth declared that there was no real proof that Mary herself was up to no good when it came to the death of Darnley. The result? Moray returned to Scotland . . . and Mary remained a prisoner in everything but name.

BESS OF HARDWICKE

Mary was moved yet *again*, this time to Tutbury Castle in Staffordshire, on the Derbyshire border. Mary'd made it clear that she'd rather be left 'bound hand and foot' in Bolton than be moved . . . but moved she was. Mary was now the responsibility of the Earl of Shrewsbury and his wife, 'Bess of Hardwicke'. In icy cold Tutbury, Mary became ill. She moved to Bess's house, Chatsworth, and Mary took up a new hobby: embroidery. Mary sent gifts of embroidery left, right and centre, including to Queen Elizabeth. Examples still survive today.

FUMING ALL ROUND

At the same time, Mary was trying to divorce Bothwell and was showing more than a little interest in the 4th Duke of Norfolk . . . which was odd, because she'd never met him! He was not only the *only* duke in England at the time – weird but true – he was also very wealthy. Elizabeth blew her top, imagining that it was a plot for Mary to strengthen her power and respectability in England. Norfolk was thrown into the Tower of London, and Mary was sent straight back to Carlisle Castle, to a smaller suite of rooms, and was forbidden to send or receive letters.

UPRISING!

One of the reasons why Elizabeth had wanted Mary moved away from Yorkshire was because it was up north . . . and up north was where most of the unhappy English Catholics were! In November, some of them rebelled. The whole thing was badly organized and had little if anything to do with supporting Catholic Mary. The result? Mary was moved even *further* south, to Coventry Castle!

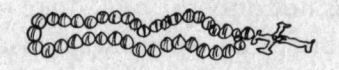

TROUBLE AT HOME

Things weren't all sweetness and light back in Scotland, either. Mary's half-brother, the Earl of Moray, was shot dead in Linlithgow on 11 June 1570. A popular tale was that he was killed by a man whose wife had caught her death of cold when Moray forced her out into the snow. The truth be told, he was assassinated by one of the Hamilton clan. The new regent was the dead Darnley's father, the 4th Earl of Lennox. Back in England, Queen Elizabeth had had a fair amount of influence in his selection.

IT'S PLOT TIME!

There then followed a series of plots involving Mary . . . whether she liked it or not. The less ambitious ones were intended to help her escape. The more ambitious ones planned to put her on the throne of England! An early plot, including a Sir Thomas Gerard, was to somehow smuggle Mary out of Chatsworth and spirit her away to the Isle of Man. There were, however, far more famous plots . . .

THE RIDOLFI PLOT

Roberto Ridolfi was an Italian banker living in England. In 1570/71, he plotted for the Spanish to invade England via Holland. The hope was that the Catholics in England would then rise up and join the Spanish invaders and, together, they'd put Mary on the English throne. King Philip II of Spain was far from convinced about the Catholics-in-England-rising-up-and-joining-the-invaders part and said that, if Ridolfi was so sure that the English Catholics were ready to rise up against Elizabeth, he'd wait until that happened and *then* send the troops in. Not that any of this mattered because the plot was soon uncovered by Elizabeth's 'secret service'. One unfortunate plotter, the Duke of Norfolk (him again), was executed for his part in it. What couldn't be proved was whether Mary herself had been involved in the plot.

THE THROCKMORTON PLOT

Like the Ridolfi plot, the Throckmorton plot got its name from one of the key plotters. No, not *that* Throckmorton. Not the Protestant Nicholas Throckmorton who'd been Queen Elizabeth I's ambassador when Mary was in the French court. *This* Throckmorton was the Catholic Francis Throckmorton. *This* Throckmorton was part of yet another plan for Catholic Spain to invade England, and for Mary to be freed and made queen. (And it's more than likely that Mary herself knew the outline of these plans at the very least.) *This* Throckmorton ended up being arrested in 1583, horribly tortured and then executed. The main problem with this plot was that the Charles Padget at the centre of it was – unknown to Throckmorton and the other plotters – a spy working for Sir Francis Walsingham, head of the English secret service.

THE PARRY PLOT

Next, the Parry plot was exposed. It turned out that a Dr Parry – who'd once had a shady job with Queen Elizabeth's government – planned to assassinate the English queen. Worse for Mary, Parry appeared to be working with a man called Thomas Morgan, Mary's own envoy in France! The last thing Mary wanted was for people to think she was involved in another plot to harm her cousin . . . She didn't want to lose what little goodwill Elizabeth might have left.

> IS THIS THE RIDOLFI OR THROCKMORTON PLOT
>
> NEITHER, MATE, WE'RE THE PARRY PLOTTERS

FEELING LOW

Mary was now at her lowest and things were about to get worse. After being in the kind care of Shrewsbury and Bess of Hardwicke, she was then put under the charge of firm-but-fair Sir Ralph Sadler. When January 1585 came around, however, Mary was not only handed over to the not-so-nice Sir Amyas Paulet but she was also moved back to Tutbury Castle, which she loathed and hated.

A TRUE PRISON

This time round, Mary's imprisonment was to be tougher than ever before. She wouldn't even be allowed in the castle grounds or courtyards to take walks, let alone go for rides. Paulet also did all he could to stop Mary sending or receiving letters, which, in the past, had been smuggled to and from her castle prisons by her servants. Mary complained that he acted as though she was a common criminal, not a crowned queen.

THE BABINGTON PLOT

Later in the year, after complaints at her treatment by the French, Mary moved to Chartley Hall, owned by the Earl of Essex. She was ill during the move, and ill for some time after. It was whilst she was there that the Babington plot, which was to lead to her downfall, unfolded. What's not clear is whether Walsingham's secret agents started the whole plot in the first place (to discredit Mary) or whether they became involved later, once the plotting was underway. What *is* clear is that, in 1586, a wealthy Catholic called Sir Anthony Babington led a plot to overthrow Queen Elizabeth with – surprise, surprise – the King of Spain . . . at least he hoped the king would be involved. From what we've seen already, that was probably a bit unlikely!

OVER A BARREL

Babington found a way of getting coded messages to and from Mary. On 16 January 1586, she was handed a message by Gilbert Gifford, who explained that it had been smuggled in using a leather pouch hidden inside a barrel of beer . . . and that she could send out secret messages in the same way. Sure enough, the messages were put in leather pouches inside barrels and smuggled in and out. What poor old Mary and the genuine plotters didn't know was that these messages were then read by Gifford and even Mary's jailer, Paulet, before being passed on. The

Protestant English knew exactly what Mary and Babington were up to.

YOU'RE NICKED!

The genuine plotters were arrested in August and Babington was taken to the Tower of London. He was soon made to confess because, thanks to Walsingham's men, his interrogators already knew all the facts anyway. He named Mary Queen of Scots as one of the conspirators.

TRICKED!

Inside her prison at Chartley, Mary herself had no idea what was going on in the outside world. When Paulet suggested they go for a ride on 11 August, she was pleased. When horsemen galloped towards them, she assumed they might be Babington plotters sent to free her. They were, in fact, the Queen of England's men there to arrest her. After a couple of weeks as a prisoner in a house at Tixall, Mary returned to Chartley, where her rooms had been thoroughly searched and many of her belongings taken. The next stop was Fotheringhay Castle in Northamptonshire which, by a twist of fate, had once belonged to a king of Scotland!

A TRIAL OF SORTS

Mary's trial began at Fotheringhay Castle on 15 October. She wore black and, riddled with rheumatism, had to be helped to her chair. She had hoped to be helped to the *throne* and was surprised and angry. Elizabeth did not attend. When Mary had a chance to speak, she accused Walsingham of creating the plot out of thin air, and Elizabeth's right-hand man, Cecil, of executing Catholics for being Catholics and nothing more. On the second day of the trial, she pointed out that not even the cleverest man in the room would have a chance of defending himself at such a trial, so what chance did she have? Everything was stacked against her.

A VERDICT IS REACHED

After the trial, and away from Fotheringhay Castle, the trial commissioners met in the Star Chamber in London. They declared Mary Queen of Scots guilty. The death sentence was passed. At the end of November, Mary spent two days writing a batch of farewell letters, which she passed on to her servants. In a number she argued that, if Elizabeth died childless, the Catholic king of Spain should get the English crown, not her own son James, unless he became a Catholic. The letters weren't delivered for many months because the poor servants themselves were imprisoned!

THE PLEAS TO SAVE HER

The protests of Mary's son, King James VI of Scotland, that his mother's life be spared were somewhat half-hearted. He was more interested in keeping in the Queen of England's good books so that he wouldn't ruin the chances of inheriting the English crown from her. The French, however, were more committed to saving their former queen. As well as many official protests from the French ambassador in London, a special ambassador was sent over by the king to plead for Mary's life. But no luck. All that was left to be done was for cousin Elizabeth to sign the death warrant.

THE INK IS DRY

Once the warrant was signed, Elizabeth didn't pass it on to her ministers. She gave the impression that she was still reluctant to let her cousin Mary die, despite everything. This was a diplomatic move on her part. In the end, her ministers decided to go ahead and arrange the execution anyway ... which meant that, if things turned nasty with the Catholic countries as a result, Elizabeth could always claim that it was *her ministers* and not *she* who'd done the dirty deed.

THE FINAL DAYS

Even Mary's jailer, Paulet, seemed saddened when the time of the execution drew nearer. He wrote that he was sad to have lived to see that unhappy day. Walsingham arranged for Bull, the executioner, to be smuggled into the castle disguised as a servant, with the executioner's axe hidden in a trunk! Knowing she was to die soon, Mary asked for her chaplain to prepare her soul for entering heaven. This was denied. Asking when she was to die, she was told, 'Tomorrow at eight o'clock'.

THE NIGHT BEFORE ...

That night, Mary divided her belongings up into piles, each to be left to different people, ranging from loyal servants to Catherine de' Medici. She arranged everything down to the last detail. This done, she lay on her bed surrounded by her loyal ladies-in-waiting, each already dressed in black, ready for what was to come. She had been Elizabeth's prisoner for over eighteen years.

... THE DAY OF EXECUTION

The day of 8 February 1587 dawned. After saying goodbye to her attendants, and brief prayers, 44-year-old Mary was led into a room with 300 spectators. She wore a black dress with a white veil, clutched a prayer book and a crucifix and held her head high. Refusing to join in a Protestant prayer – saying that she was a Catholic and would 'spend [her] blood in defence of it' – she prayed out loud for her son James VI and for Queen Elizabeth. Then, following tradition, she forgave Bull, the executioner, and his assistants. Then they undressed her down to her dark red petticoat. It was also tradition that the executioner keep any of the ornaments she'd been wearing, but she asked that the rosaries tucked in her belt be given to particular friends. The executioner would be given money instead. Although many of her female attendants were in flood of tears by now, Mary seemed almost calm.

THE FINAL BLOW

With a white cloth wrapped around her head, a bit like a turban, Mary Queen of Scots knelt on a cushion and laid her neck on the block. Bull's first blow chopped the back of her *head* instead of her neck. (Some people claimed they heard Mary whisper 'Sweet Jesus'.) The second blow almost cut right through her neck, but not quite. The axe had to be used a third time but, even then, the story is not over.

AN EXTRAORDINARY END

Bull lifted Mary's severed head high by the hair, crying 'God Save the Queen' but – to his amazement and the crowd's horror – the head fell to the ground. What the executioner was left clutching was a brown wig! Mary's head on the floor had short, grey hair . . . and her lips were still moving, some say in silent prayer, for about a quarter of an hour. If that wasn't bad enough, Mary's pet dog, Skye, now appeared from under Mary's petticoat where it'd been hiding, and refused to leave its lifeless mistress.

LAID TO REST

So, with Mary Queen of Scots well-and-truly dead, this book is at an end. Queen Elizabeth pretended to be outraged that the execution had been carried out without her say-so, but few were convinced by this act. She did, indeed, die childless and Mary's son James, as well as being King James VI of Scotland, became King James I of England in 1603. Mary was originally buried in Peterborough but James had her body brought to Westminster Abbey in great splendour. She had wanted to be buried in France, but Elizabeth had forbidden this.

AN AFTERTHOUGHT

There's one weird fact that may not have occurred to you but, if you go back through the book, you'll see it's true. Despite the fact that each played such an important part in the other's life and, in the case of Mary, her eventual death, Queen Elizabeth I of England and Mary Queen of Scots never actually met each other face-to-face. Not even once. Ever.

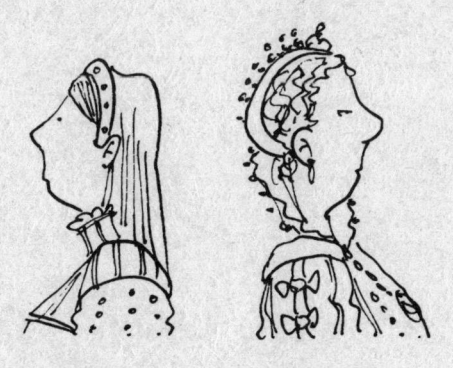

TIMELINE
At home and abroad

1491	Henry is born at Greenwich Palace.
1492	*Columbus almost 'discovers' America, actually Caribbean islands, but thinks it's China.*
1495-98	*Leonardo da Vinci paints 'The Last Supper'.*
1509	Henry marries Catherine of Aragon. Becomes King of England.
1512	*Michelangelo finishes painting the ceiling of the Sistine Chapel.*
1516	Birth of 'Bloody' Mary.
1519	Birth of Henry's illegitimate son, Henry Fitzroy.
1520	The Field of the Cloth of Gold.
1530	Cardinal Thomas Wolsey dies (before he can get the chop).
1533	Henry secretly marries Anne Boleyn. Archbishop Thomas Cranmer divorces Henry from Catherine. *The Spanish conquer the Inca Empire in Peru.* Princess (later Queen) Elizabeth is born. *Inca Empire (of Peru) conquered by Spanish.*
1534	*Turks capture Baghdad and Mesopotamia (now Iraq)*
1535	Thomas More executed.
1536	Catherine of Aragon dies (of natural causes). Anne Boleyn executed. Dissolution of the smaller monasteries. Henry marries Jane Seymour.
1536-7	Pilgrimage of Grace rebellion.

	Dissolution of the larger monasteries begins.

	Dissolution of the larger monasteries begins.
	Birth of Prince Edward, the future Edward VI.
	Jane Seymour dies.
1538	Thomas à Becket's tomb destroyed at Canterbury.
	Pope excommunicates Henry.
	The name 'America' used for the first time.
	First flintlock weapons used.
1540	Henry marries Anne of Cleves in January . . . and divorces her in July.
	Thomas Cromwell executed.
	Henry marries Catherine Howard.
1542	Catherine Howard executed.
	Mary Stuart is born in December.
	Mary Stuart becomes Queen of Scots at one week old when her father dies.
1543	Henry VIII marries Catherine Parr.
	Henry VIII arranges engagement between Mary Stuart and his son Edward.
	Mary Stuart crowned at Stirling Castle.
1545	*The* Mary Rose *sinks.*
1546	*Michelangelo appointed architect of St Peter's in Rome.*
1547	Henry VIII dies, Edward becomes King Edward VI.
	English defeat Scots at Pinkie Cleugh.
1548	Mary leaves Scotland for France.
1553	Edward VI dies. Lady Jane Grey is queen for nine days before Mary Tudor ('Bloody Mary') becomes Queen of England.
1558	Mary Stuart marries the dauphin, Francis.
	England loses Calais to France.
	Mary I dies, Elizabeth becomes Queen of England.
1559	Mary Stuart becomes Queen of France too.
1560	Mary's mother dies. So does Mary's husband, now King Francis II of France.

1561	Mary Stuart returns to Scotland. *Sir Francis Bacon is born.*
1564	*William Shakespeare born in Stratford-upon-Avon.*
1565	Mary Stuart marries Lord Darnley.
1566	Rizzio is murdered. Mary gives birth to son James.
1567	Lord Darnley is murdered. Mary marries Bothwell, surrenders to the Protestants and is taken to Lochleven. Son James is made King James VI of Scotland.
1568	Mary escapes from Lochleven and flees to England, becoming a virtual prisoner for the rest of her life.
1571	Ridolfi plot.
1577	Drake sets off on his around-the-world voyage.
1580	Drake returns from his circumnavigation (a big word for the above).
1583	Throckmorton plot.
1586	Mary is arrested and tried for her part in the Babington Plot.
1587	Mary Queen of Scots beheaded at Fotheringhay.
1588	Spanish Armada defeated.
1589	*William Lee invents machine for knitting stockings.*
1593	*Playwright Marlowe murdered in Deptford tavern.*
1596	*Tomatoes introduced to England.* *First water closets (WCs) installed in England*
1601	Essex beheaded.
1603	Elizabeth I dies. Mary Stuart's son, James VI of Scotland becomes James I of England.

INDEX

Act of Succession 35, 36, 40, 76
Anne of Cleves *see* Cleves
Aragon, Catherine of 7–10, 13, 19–24, 27, 29, 30, 34–40, 44, 62, 65, 67, 79, 136, 175
Armada 93, 98–109, 177
Arran, Earl of 86, 121–8, 148
Babington, Sir Anthony 90, 166–7, 177
Bacon, Sir Francis 113, 177
bagpipes 145
beard, the innocent 38
Beaton, Cardinal 121–7, 146
beheading 1, 2, 9, 10, 28, 38, 48, 66–7, 70, 78, 92, 96, 108, 110, 149, 170–2, 177
Bloody Mary *see* Mary I
Boleyn, Anne 21–8, 34–8, 51, 136, 175
boots, as rations 96
Bothwell, Earl of 88, 89, 148, 152, 154–6, 159–70, 177
bowls 98
Calvin, John 117
Calvinism 117, 146
cardinals 1, 10, 11, 17, 18, 21, 23–32, 75, 121–8, 131, 146, 175
Catherine de' Medici 126, 129, 132, 137, 140, 170
Catherine of Aragon *see* Aragon
Catholic Church 1, 11, 14, 23, 30–1, 47, 117, 123, 126–7, 136
Charles V 13–15, 23–4, 48–9, 53
Cleves, Anne of 50, 69, 176
Cranmer, Thomas 30–1, 35, 55, 75, 175
Cromwell, Thomas 30, 35, 41, 48, 49, 50–1
Darnley, Lord 87–9, 141, 150–4, 159–63, 177

Dee, Dr John 82
doctors 1, 82, 153
dog 92, 172
Don Carlos of Spain 140, 150
Drake, Sir Francis 94, 97–101, 107, 177
Dudley, Lord 87, 105, 150
earls 21, 64, 86, 103, 105, 108, 110, 121–6, 128–9, 141, 144, 148–51, 157–66
Edinburgh 88, 112, 127–8, 138, 142, 144, 147–8, 152–6
Edward VI 46, 53, 55, 68–9, 70, 73, 74, 75–6 176
Elizabeth of York 2, 5, 6
Essex, Earl of 103, 105, 110, 166
execution, *see* beheading
Field of the Cloth of Gold 12, 175
Francis I of France 12–15, 48–9
Francis II of France 85, 126, 129, 132, 134, 138–41, 155, 176
Golden Hind 97
Greenwich Palace 5, 8, 46, 61, 175
Grey, Lady Jane 55, 77, 176
Hampton Court 10, 46, 65, 69
Hatfield 64, 73, 75, 80
Henry VII 2, 3, 5, 138
Henry Fitzroy, Duke of Richmond 20, 21–2, 36, 40, 67, 70
heresy 1, 20, 30, 77
Holbein, Hans 48–9
Holyrood Palace 112, 127, 144–5, 151, 155
Howard, Catherine 51–2, 69, 70, 78, 176
Ireland 48, 61, 104, 107–9
James IV of Scotland 141
James VI of Scotland and I of England 156, 160, 169, 171–2, 177
Knox, John 145–6, 150

Luther, Martin 20
marmalade 132–3
Mary I 20, 36, 40, 44, 53, 55, 62, 65, 67, 70, 74, 76–80, 83, 85, 176
Mary of Guise 119, 130, 134, 138
Mary Rose 16, 176
monasteries 41–5, 54, 175, 176
More, Sir Thomas 29, 31, 35, 37–8, 175
Pale, the 109
Parr, Catherine 53–4, 70, 73–6, 176
Parry, Dr 164
Philip II of Spain 77, 98, 101, 102, 105, 163
plague 25–6
plots 15, 44, 78, 87, 90–1, 110–1, 114, 147–8, 153, 160–1, 163–8, 177
Pope 1, 10, 14–5, 20, 22–5, 31–4, 44–8, 62, 72, 77, 85, 117, 123, 176
potatoes 94, 96, 100
Protestants 48, 69, 77, 85–6, 93, 98, 100, 104, 108, 117–8, 123, 125–7, 138, 144–8, 151, 155, 158–6, 164, 167, 171, 175
Raleigh, Sir Walter 94–5, 100, 107, 113

rebellions 17, 43, 110, 175
Rizzio, David 88, 151–2, 177
Ridolfi, Roberto 90, 163–4, 177
scurvy 97
Seymour, Jane 38–40, 43, 46–8, 54, 65, 68–9, 175, 176
Shakespeare, William 84, 113, 177
Stirling Castle 125, 129, 151–2, 154, 176
Throckmorton, Francis 90, 164
Throckmorton, Sir Nicholas 142, 147
tobacco 96
Tower of London 8, 37, 66, 68, 70, 75, 161, 167
treason 35, 38, 47, 51, 149
Tudor rose 5
Tudors 2
ulcers 54
Valois, Catherine de 3–4
Valor Ecclesiasticus 14
Wales 4, 5, 61, 108
Walsingham 114, 164, 166–8, 170
Westminster Abbey 8, 50, 172
wigs 92, 109, 110, 171
Wolsey, Cardinal Thomas 10, 11, 24, 29–31, 175

GET A LIFE!
QUEEN VICTORIA

PHILIP ARDAGH

Victoria's first name was actually Alexandrina. She was named after Tsar Alexander I of Russia.

Victoria had nine children, forty grandchildren, and numerous Persian cats, collie dogs and pet pigeons.

After an assassination attempt, she carried a chainmail-lined parasol.

She created the Victoria Cross – medals made from Russian guns captured during the Crimean War – as the highest award for valour.

Collect all the GET A LIFE! titles

The prices shown below are correct at the time of going to press. However Macmillan Publishers reserve the right to show new retail prices on covers which may differ from those previously advertised.

Julius Caesar	0 330 37507 5	£2.99
Queen Victoria	0 330 37510 5	£2.99
Oliver Cromwell	0 330 37572 5	£2.99
Marie Curie	0 330 37571 7	£2.99
Napoleon	0 330 48089 8	£2.99

All Macmillan titles can be ordered at your local bookshop or are available by post from:

**Book Service by Post
P0 Box 29, Douglas, Isle of Man IM99 1BO**

Credit cards accepted. For details:
Telephone: 01624 675137
Fax: 01624 670923
E-mail: bookshop@enterprise.net

Free postage and packing in the UK.
Overseas customers: add £1 per book (paperback)
and £3 per book (hardback).